UNIVERSAL DIFFERENCE

Universal Difference

Feminism and the Liberal Undecidability of 'Women'

Kate Nash
Lecturer in Sociology
University of East Anglia
Norwich

First published in Great Britain 1998 by
MACMILLAN PRESS LTD
Houndmills, Basingstoke, Hampshire RG21 6XS and London
Companies and representatives throughout the world

A catalogue record for this book is available from the British Library.

ISBN 0–333–72116–0

First published in the United States of America 1998 by
ST. MARTIN'S PRESS, INC.,
Scholarly and Reference Division,
175 Fifth Avenue, New York, N.Y. 10010

ISBN 0–312–21004–3

Library of Congress Cataloging-in-Publication Data
Nash, Kate, 1958–
Universal difference : feminism and the liberal undecidability of
women / Kate Nash.
    p. cm.
Includes bibliographical references and index.
ISBN 0–312–21004–3 (cloth)
1. Feminist theory. 2. Women and democracy. 3. Liberalism.
4. Feminism. I. Title.
HQ1190.N36 1997
305.42'01—dc21   97–28032
                                                    CIP

This book is printed on paper suitable for recycling and made from fully managed and
sustained forest sources.

10   9   8   7   6   5   4   3   2   1
07 06 05 04 03 02 01 00 99 98

Printed in Great Britain by
The Ipswich Book Company Ltd
Ipswich, Suffolk

To my mother

Contents

Acknowledgements

I would like to thank everyone who has discussed the ideas in this book with me, especially Ernesto Laclau, Vicky Randall, Anne Phillips, Aletta Norval, Jelica Sumic-Riha and Simon Thompson, who have all read chapters or, in some cases, the entire manuscript when it was a doctoral thesis.

I would also like to thank colleagues and students at City University, Essex University and the University of East Anglia for stimulating thought while I was writing it, especially Ali Rattansi, Carolyn Vogler, Stephan Feuchtwang, David Howarth, Anna-Marie Smith, Sue Golding, Tony Clohesy, Barnor Hesse, Farish Ahmad-Noor, Richard Bellamy, Alan Scott, Roberta Sassattelli, Martin Hollis, Augus Ross and Tim O'Hagan. I would especially like to thank Michèle Barrett who has always been inspiring by her encouragement to question received wisdom.

I am more thankful than I can say to Zoé Nash, Maryam Najand, Anne-Marie Fortier and Neil Washbourne who have given support and encouragement, as well as good ideas and much needed relief from the task of producing the thesis and then the book; their goodwill in sustaining me to the very end of the project has been invaluable and has made it much more enjoyable than it otherwise would have been.

The arguments presented here will not meet with the agreement of all those who have helped me, but without you I probably wouldn't have done it as I have, and maybe I wouldn't have done it at all.

The Economic and Social Research Council funded the doctoral research on which this book is based.

Is the differential treatment of women and men part of the sorry history of liberal democracy, or built into their very foundations? Does liberal democracy have to turn itself into something other – an alternative to liberal democracy – in order to deal with sexual inequality? Or can the inadequacies and inequalities be redressed with some future, but still liberal, democracy?

1 Introduction

DEMOCRATIC CONSIDERATIONS OF LIBERALISM

This study is concerned with the question of the universal principles of liberalism and the extent to which they are applicable to women in their specificity *as* women. It is, therefore, concerned with the current feminist questioning of liberalism's universality, but it will take a rather more sympathetic view of the value of liberalism to feminism than most of the recent literature on the subject. As it will be one of the aims of this study to show, the relationship between feminism and liberalism has been long and, though not exactly joyful, ambivalent rather than unhappy. The study will argue that this ambivalence has been highly productive for feminism and has the potential to continue to be so in the future.

Most contemporary feminist political theorists see liberalism as unequivocally incompatible with feminism as a project and argue that we must break free from its categories and principles. In particular, they argue, a feminism that uses the universal principles of liberalism to try to gain equality with men and liberty from subordination to men is doomed to failure. It will only ever contribute to the advancement of those women who mimic men and, since no women can do so beyond a certain point, ultimately it will fail them too. We shall look at these feminist critiques of liberalism as essentially masculinist in detail in chapter 2, but in order to introduce the debate in which this study is situated we shall look briefly here at their main points and at the much less extensive and rather more tentative feminist case for the rehabilitation of liberalism. Questions concerning the use of liberalism also have a wider resonance given the recent socialist rethinking of liberal categories and principles, so we shall consider the problems raised by the feminist critique of liberalism as masculinist for these approaches; if these feminists are right, then any approach that appropriates liberal terms may be masculinist too.

According to feminist critiques of liberalism as masculinist, it is by no means an historical accident that women have not been treated as the free and equal individuals of liberalism; it is rather that those individuals are necessarily, by definition, masculine. This means that liberal principles can only be applied to masculine activities, those in

1

which rational, detached agents are able to calculate means and ends, draw up legally binding contracts and so on; to focus only on such activities means excluding from view those feminine activities which do not conform to this model, those which involve non-rational care and incalculable reciprocity, for example. To use liberal principles, then, means to marginalise activities and characteristics which are the province of women *as* women. So, far from showing how justice for women is to be achieved, liberalism either results in ignoring women's specificity altogether or, if feminists insist on applying liberal principles inappropriately to women's lives, to the corrosion of forms of life on which embodied humans actually depend and which made the illusion of liberal individualism possible in the first place (Fox-Genovese, 1991). Furthermore it is argued that the public/private distinction, which is absolutely central to the liberal tradition, rules women, and those aspects of social life that have traditionally been the concern of women, as outside the bounds of political consideration. Although feminist critics of liberalism as masculine do not necessarily argue that no difference at all should be made between public and private, they insist, against what they see as the liberal tradition, that the domestic sphere must not be seen as non-political (Pateman, 1989b, pp. 134–6).

What most concerns those feminists for whom an outright rejection of liberalism is less appealing is that its ideal, abstract individual has been extremely effective as a means by which women have begun to extricate themselves from of the subordination to which traditional 'womanly' identities and forms of life have contributed. Are we to give up such a powerful weapon, especially when it would seem that we have nothing comparable to put in its place? As Phillips points out, liberal theorists like Will Kymlicka have argued for group rights on the impeccably liberal grounds of individual freedom (Phillips, 1993a, p. 118; Kymlicka, 1989). One of the conclusions of this study will be that since liberalism began to be democratised in the nineteenth century it has actually gone some way towards recognising and supporting the rights of women *as* women, albeit half-heartedly. In practice, then, liberal-democracy does not permit only the freedom and equality of detached masculine individuals; in a democratised liberalism there is at least the possibility of the equal freedom of other categories of persons too. This possibility will be further discussed in the Conclusion. The difficulty that is then raised concerning the tension between the recognition of group rights and those of the individual will be also be discussed in the Conclusion.

Another main area of worry for those whom we might call feminist revisionists is the rejection of the liberal public/private distinction. There are, in fact, two disputes here. The first links up with the previous concern over the rejection of the abstract individual insofar as, according to some revisionists, we should be concerned to extend the liberal right to privacy to women as individuals, rather than to displace or reform the public/private distinction altogether (Okin, 1991, pp. 87–90; Kymlicka, 1990, pp. 261–2; Phillips, 1991, p. 109). Again, this study is supportive of this point and again it shows how, in practice, a democratised liberalism has instituted such rights, at least up to a point.

The second area of dispute concerns the question of the liberal division between public and private as that between state and civil society and the extent to which this division can be separated from the gendered division between the state and civil society as the public sphere and the household as the private sphere. This issue is enormously complex and it will be the focus of much of the analysis of particular liberal and feminist projects throughout the course of this study. It is of particular contemporary interest since much radical rethinking of liberal-democracy, stimulated by the fall of socialism in Western and Eastern Europe, along with the rise in importance of the new social movements, and that of the New Right and its neo-liberal agenda, has been concerned with the limits of the state and the revitalising of democratic politics at the level of the state and of a pluralist civil society. Insofar as these projects work with certain liberal categories, whether acknowledged as such or not, the extent to which they are compatible with feminism may be said to depend on how far liberalism can accommodate women's concerns *as* women.

The rethinking of socialism represented by the work of Paul Hirst, John Keane, and Ernesto Laclau and Chantal Mouffe has a number of themes in common deriving from the rejection of Marxism on which it is based. These projects are all principally concerned with politics and with the analysis of the social as a contingent, concrete set of conditions rather than with trying to produce a scientific understanding of the laws of development of history which could provide a guide for the transformation of society as a totality. They are all concerned with how the principles and institutions of contemporary liberal-democratic capitalism might be extended to provide conditions of greater equality, liberty and democracy.

Paul Hirst is most explicit in this respect, arguing that his theory of associative democracy 'extends and enhances liberalism and does not seek to supersede it' (Hirst, 1994, p. 19). It would extend individual choice, for Hirst the cornerstone of liberalism, by substantially limiting state power and building up voluntary, largely self-regulating associations to manage economic conditions and provide welfare in a more democratic and pluralist way than is currently the case in a society governed by a bureaucratic, centralised and homogenising state.

An important question for Hirst is that of individuals' rights within the associations they form, since clearly associations cannot be said to extend choice if they act in authoritarian ways towards their members. He is principally concerned in this respect with the negative liberty of liberal individualism and he supposes that this can be ensured by the legal 'right to exit' from any association of which an individual is a member (pp. 50–2). However, Hirst gives no consideration at all to the feminist concerns over whether women can be liberal individuals. In effect, his voluntary associations are contractual and, according to the feminist critique of liberalism as masculinist, the groups in which women are particularly implicated, notably the family, are not fundamentally of this type and cannot, therefore, be regulated by liberal principles of individual rights. In effect Hirst has argued for the extension of the private sphere of civil society in order to counteract the power of the state without considering the public/private distinction within civil society itself, that between the household and other social institutions.

A similar problem arises in the arguments of John Keane for a democratisation of both state and civil society. Although Keane seems deliberately to avoid the use of liberal language, without stating his reasons, in arguing for a clear separation between the state and civil society in order to ensure pluralism and citizens' freedom he is clearly retracing familiar liberal themes:

> The secret of liberty ... is the division of decision-making powers into a variety of institutions within and between the state. The maximisation of citizens' liberty entails the enlargement of their choices – particularly among those presently worse off.
>
> (Keane, 1988, p. 13)

Like Hirst, Keane argues for the devolving of state power to voluntary, self-determining groups in civil society in order to provide for local needs, but he also argues for a revitalising of democracy at the level of the state, with political parties which positively encourage internal debate and are responsive to new social movements (pp. 141–3) and a reformed parliament with greater control over the state (pp. 170–5). Keane does directly address issues raised by feminists in recent years, arguing that the democratisation of civil society must take place through 'social struggles and public policy initiatives' that will curtail the power of capital and of white, heterosexual men in order to enable all citizens to participate equally (p. 14). However, he does not specifically address the issues raised by the feminist critique of liberalism as masculinist. According to Keane, civil society has the potential to become 'a non-state sphere comprising a plurality of public spheres – productive units, *households*, voluntary organisations and community-based services – which are legally guaranteed and self-organising' (p. 14; emphasis added). To describe households 'as public spheres' sounds distinctly odd given the history of the family as the place of privacy in liberal-democracies, and raises both strategic questions about how they could be transformed in this way as well as normative ones about whether, or to what extent, personal relationships should be opened up to public scrutiny in the same way as other social and economic relationships (see Okin, 1991, on this question). In other words, Keane again fails to address the question of the specificity of the privacy of the domestic sphere and whether the terms of 'masculine' political theory can be extended to deal with it.

Laclau's and Mouffe's post-Marxism has informed much of the work of this study insofar as it takes liberalism as a hegemonic project, rather than simply as a political philosophy, and a feminist argument for their theory of radical democracy is developed in detail in the Conclusion. For Laclau and Mouffe radical democracy involves the extension of the principles of liberty and equality hegemonic in liberal-democracy, the institution of the maximum achievable degree of equality and liberty for all and the – never realisable – aspiration towards complete universal equality and liberty (Laclau and Mouffe, 1985, ch. 4). Unlike Hirst and Keane, they have little to say about the social and political institutions by means of which this is to be achieved, though in later work Mouffe does argue for the importance of procedural democracy and of a public/private distinction in order to ensure pluralism and individual liberty (Mouffe, 1993, p. 62).

In my view the vaguer notion of radical democracy is to be preferred to the more programmatic versions of Hirst and Keane because this theory is closer to what Keane dismisses as the old socialist idea of democracy as a means to greater equality rather than as an end in itself (Keane, 1988, p. 25). Although it is clearly important to consider practical suggestions for the reform of liberal-democracy, it is not at all evident that the suggestions Hirst and Keane make, particularly those concerning the importance of the voluntary and self-regulating

aspects of the institutions of civil society which would inevitably legitimise restrictions on membership of those institutions, could prevent
the increased marginalisation of the poor with which both are at least
partly concerned. It is not that Laclau and Mouffe make concrete suggestions about how this is to be avoided – on the contrary, they make
few concrete suggestions at all – but the advantage of their idea of
radical democracy is that it contains the idea of greater equality as
well as liberty such that so long as there is recognised inequality,
democracy cannot be said to have been achieved. The marginalisation
of the poor cannot then be legitimately ignored as it can on Keane's
and Hirst's theories, however well-intentioned these theorists themselves may be.

Of those attempting to think liberal-democracy from an avowedly
post-Marxist point of view, only Chantal Mouffe directly addresses the
question of the feminist critique of liberalism as masculinist in relation to the theory of radical democracy she worked out initially with
Ernesto Laclau. In an article titled 'Feminism, Citizenship and Radical Democratic Politics', Mouffe discusses the feminist critique of the
liberal individual as masculinist and agrees with Carole Pateman that:

> the modern category of the individual has been constructed in a manner
> that postulates a universalist, homogeneous 'public' that relegates
> all particularity and difference to the 'private', and that this has very
> negative consequences for women.
>
> (p. 81)

This does not mean, however, according to Mouffe, that we should
abandon the universalist principles of citizenship in favour a gender-
differentiated citizenship in the way that Pateman proposes. It is important, according to Mouffe, that all citizens identify with the principles
of equality and liberty – they form what Mouffe calls the 'grammar'
of liberal democracy, it is what we as citizens have in common –
these principles must, therefore, be universal and radical democratic
citizenship must be gender-neutral. On the other hand, what guarantees pluralism for Mouffe is that these principles are open to citizens'
own interpretations; in fact, politics *is* the struggle between different
interpretations of these common universal principles (pp. 70–1). A
possible feminist interpretation of these principles is that women must
be treated *differently* from men in order to achieve equality and, following her acceptance of the feminist critique of the liberal individual
as masculinist, Mouffe herself endorses this interpretation (p. 82). But

here there would seem to be an inconsistency in her argument; if, on occasion, the universal principle of equality were interpreted and instituted differently for women and men, then radical democratic citizenship itself would be differentiated by sex (see Nash, forthcoming, for an elaboration of this argument). Mouffe herself is anxious to avoid this conclusion because she sees it as essentialist, as presupposing a fixed and foundational sexual difference which will limit in advance the articulation of identities where the possibility of multiple and contextually sensitive links between identities is the condition of a radical democratic political project. This problem will be addressed again in the Conclusion, where it will be argued that it is possible, and necessary, to recognise women's specificity from a radical democratic perspective without thereby committing oneself to metaphysical sexual difference.

Finally, as one of those who is engaged in rethinking liberal-democracy from a socialist *and* feminist perspective, we must consider the civic republicanism of Anne Phillips. Like the other socialists we have looked at, she is concerned to revitalise democracy in order to accommodate the pluralism of contemporary society. For this reason she argues for the liberal-democratic distinction between political and non-political. According to Phillips, we should reserve the term 'political' for democratic activities in the public sphere in which 'we are faced with people who are different and have to work out with them our common and shared concerns' (Phillips, 1991, p. 117). It is not that feminists should thereby give up the activities they currently think of as political in civil society and in the domestic sphere, but rather that in pluralist societies the only hope of solidarity and social transformation is through democratic dialogue and decision-making in a sphere in which all are represented.

Phillips' version of democracy is, then, even narrower than Hirst's or Keane's, focusing only on political reform at the level of the state. However, as a feminist, Phillips does consider the possibility of women's participation in democracy, arguing that actually, with their domestic responsibilities, women were ill-served by socialist feminist ideals of participatory democracy since they were *less* likely than men to be able to meet the demands of such institutions. In order to ensure women's participation in representative democracy, she argues for political parties to set quotas for women and other minorities. It is important to note, however, that her argument here is that quotas should be set in order to realise equal opportunities for women to participate in government, not that women should be included in democratic institutions in order to represent women in general: Phillips is very clear that in a pluralist society where each individual has many different identities, such group representation is impossible (pp. 73–4). It would seem, then, that her argument has no *necessary* consequences for women's equality outside the narrow sphere she designates as political, even if there happens to be an empirical link between quotas and greater social and economic equality for women. In this respect, although Phillips' argument that quotas are necessary to end sex discrimination in political parties is convincing, her view of democracy is again less satisfactory than Laclau's and Mouffe's more general theory, oriented as it is towards increasing equality.

According to Phillips, then, liberal democracy as it stands is not currently accommodating of women's specificity as women; she agrees with the feminist critics of liberalism as masculinist that it excludes women from political participation and also from equal citizenship rights with men (Phillips, 1993a), but for Phillips it is an open question whether or not liberalism could be democratised to the point where women could recognise themselves in its terms. It is with this question that this study is concerned.

LIBERALISM AS PHILOSOPHY IN PRACTICE

Most of the literature criticising liberalism as masculinist approaches it from a broadly philosophical perspective, analysing concepts and distinctions in the canonical texts of liberal political philosophy. Although this study does look at texts, it approaches them in a rather different way. The principal aim is to examine liberalism *in practice* rather than just as a set of ideas: to look at the way liberal principles have been used and how its categories have been produced, reproduced and modified in social and political action. It approaches liberalism as 'the dominant ideology of the West' (Arblaster, 1984, p. 6), embedded in changing social and political institutions since it first gained legitimacy in the seventeenth century. Above all, it is concerned with changes in liberal practices throughout modernity and particularly with the extent to which feminists have been able to modify liberalism so that women might be taken into account within its categories and principles. Taking a long historical view, it is inclined towards optimism about the feminist use of liberalism, while others tend to be a good deal more pessimistic. It is hoped that the reader will find the optimism well founded by the analysis made in the following pages.

Discourse Theory

At the most general level, that is, as a characterisation of social reality, the study takes discourse theory as its starting point. According to discourse theory, the very possibility of perception, thought and action depends on the structuring of *meaning*, prior to any experience. On this approach, social reality is, then, constructed according to the rules of language: it is meaningful in the way that language is meaningful. Social reality is not given to experience and then named; rather it is the naming that makes reality what it is (Laclau, 1993a).

For the purposes of this study, two aspects of discourse theory are particularly important. First, following Michel Foucault, it is important to look at the occurrence of particular articulations of terms in their historical contexts; it is important to grasp the conditions of existence of a particular statement in its relation to other statements (Foucault, 1972, pp. 21–7). This conception of discourse encourages us to trace the detail of historical changes in the meaning and significance of what might, if they were lifted out of their historical context, look like the same terms. Although liberalism always turns on the same set of terms – liberty, equality, individual, public, private – they have very different meanings in different historical contexts. Second, however, breaking with Foucault's rather confusing distinction between discourse and the extra-discursive, *all* social reality is seen as discursively constructed. While it may on occasion be useful to distinguish between language – written documents, speeches, conversation, and so on – and the social and political institutions in which language is used, such a distinction can only be analytic, it cannot be ontological. Social and political practices are meaningful and they are, therefore, discursive; they are produced in language as much as language is produced in social and political institutions (Laclau and Mouffe, 1985, pp. 105–9).

It is because social reality is discursively produced that the study of the texts of liberal political philosophy can offer insights into the categories and principles which contribute to the production and reproduction of social and political practices. However, this raises two further methodological questions which must be dealt with before we can look at how the study is to proceed. First, how are texts to be read or interpreted? And second, what is the precise relation between the texts of political philosophy and social and political institutions?

Deconstruction

The most appropriate method for the interpretation of the texts of liberal political philosophy for our purposes here is deconstruction, as developed by Jacques Derrida; like the feminist critique of liberalism which is the starting point of the study, one of its primary concerns is the binary oppositions of Western thought. It is therefore a useful tool with which to examine how the oppositions feminists have identified as contributing to the exclusion of women's specificity from liberalism have been constructed in liberal texts; in particular, the opposition between public and private and its association with that between masculine and feminine. However, the emphasis of deconstruction is very different from that of most feminist critiques of liberalism.

While most feminists readily acknowledge that liberalism has, at least sometimes, been used to advance the position of women, once they begin to criticise liberalism for its 'masculinism', for the way in which it excludes the specificity of women's embodiment and historical position in the gendered division of labour, they repress this recognition. For example, in one of the first feminist articles on liberalism, Teresa Brennan and Carole Pateman acknowledge the potential of early liberalism, with its universal principles of liberty and equality, to open up new possibilities for women and they note that there are ambiguities in the way in which Hobbes and Locke position women as sometimes included in these universal principles and sometimes excluded from them (Brennan and Pateman, 1979). Brennan and Pateman are unable, however, to incorporate their recognition of these ambiguities into their analysis; they must be left aside as irrelevant. What is really significant for them, as for the other feminists we will look at in chapter 2, is how women are *excluded* from liberal principles because of their positioning in the private domestic sphere, and not the ambiguities of their positioning in both public and private. They therefore push these ambiguities aside to focus on exclusion. From the point of view of Derridean deconstruction, however, it is precisely such ambiguities, the impossibility of making clear-cut either/or distinctions, that must be taken into account. There are no cases of simple exclusion.

It is difficult to sum up Derrida's work – it is very complex and is always dependent on the close reading of particular texts – but there is one theme that dominates it: Derrida is committed to exposing the way in which philosophy dreams of presence, and the way in which that dream will never be realised because it is inherently impossible. Philosophy dreams of presence in that it would like its most important concepts to be absolutely determinate, self-identical, capable of rigorous definition and non-contradictory in meaning. This dream cannot be realised according to Derrida because of the way in which presence, or identity, always depends on difference, which makes it simultaneously possible and impossible. Paradoxically, it is the inconsistencies and ambiguities in texts which enable the *illusion* of presence.

This basic thesis can be understood at various levels of abstraction. At the most abstract level Rodolphe Gasche explains it in the following way. In order to be determinate, that is to be anything at all, a concept must have an outside, it must be bounded. There is no possibility of a concept appearing alone, without relation to at least one other in which it is in a dichotomous relationship.[1] But if this is so, it must be that the concept which allows the determinacy of the original concept is necessary to that original concept and so, in some way or another, it must be included within it. The other against which it necessarily defines itself in order to be itself is simultaneously outside of the concept, as the condition of its possibility, and inside it, as the condition of its impossibility (Gasche, 1986, pp. 187–8). The impossibility of separating outside from inside which is the condition of possibility, and impossibility, of presence or identity, Derrida calls undecidability (Derrida, 1988, pp. 116–17).

There are no cases of simple exclusion, then, because each side of a binary opposition depends on the other; each side is simultaneously outside and inside the other. According to Derrida, the impossibility of the self-presence of philosophical concepts is obscured in the case of binary oppositions by the way in which one of the terms is privileged over the other. One term is seen as offering universal, necessary truth while the other is understood to be derivative or corrupting of truth and necessity, a kind of contingent addition to the first concept, on which it must have no important effects. There are historical reasons for the particular hierarchical arrangement of binary oppositions which it is one of the tasks of deconstruction to discover (Derrida, 1988, p. 137; Gasche, 1986, p. 171). The project in deconstructing a text is to unravel the necessary relation of the degraded term to the privileged one and to uncover the repression of the former in the latter.

According to Derrida there is no method as such according to which one must proceed in order to uncover the trace of the other in the same, though this 'does not rule out a certain marching order' (Derrida, 1981a, p. 271). There can be no method that is applied mechanically to a text because deconstruction consists in following the 'lines of force and forces of rupture that are localisable in the discourse to be deconstructed' (Derrida, 1981b, p. 82). Deconstruction consists in unravelling the undecidability in the relations between concepts that are proper to the text in question. Nevertheless, Derrida does make some recommendations concerning how to proceed in uncovering these relations. He suggests first reversing the values of the terms of binary oppositions – privileging the one that has been downgraded as unnecessary. Then the next step becomes possible, the restoration of the characteristics or traits which have been repressed in this degraded term to their generality. That is, deconstruction shows how characteristics which are supposedly proper only to the degraded term and excluded from the privileged one are actually necessary to the constitution of both and of the difference between them. These characteristics Derrida calls 'undecidables' (Derrida, 1981b, p. 43).

Undecidables are at the same time proper to particular texts and generalised in the history of Western metaphysics (Derrida, 1981b, pp. 41–3; Gasche, 1986, pp. 171–2). They can, therefore, be found in texts other than those in which they were initially discovered. It is for this reason that I think it is justified to adopt a slightly different approach, a slightly different 'marching order' from the one which Derrida recommends. In this study I shall make a close deconstructive reading of three texts of liberal political philosophy and identify there the way in which the term 'women' functions as an undecidable, constitutive of the central opposition of liberalism, that between public and private. The term 'women' functions as such in different ways in different texts, but broadly speaking it is able to do so because it has the characteristics Derrida has identified in the undecidable 'hymen'. 'Hymen' has the double meaning in Latin (as it has been translated from the original Greek) of both 'membrane' and 'marriage'; it means 'between' both in the sense of fusion and of separation. As such, according to Derrida's reading of Mallarmé's *La Mimique* in which 'hymen' was first identified, it describes the neither/nor of the mime; neither original, nor imitation 'it is located between present acts that don't take place' (Derrida, 1981a, p. 220) In fact, Derrida suggests, the double meaning of 'hymen' is useful only for economy; it could be replaced by 'identity' or 'difference' (that is, by both of them together – perhaps it would be better to write 'identity/difference') with no loss except that of economic condensation or accumulation: 'It is the 'between', whether it names fusion or separation, that carries the force of the operation' (p. 220).

Derridean deconstruction will be used, then, to show how the ambiguities feminists frequently acknowledge and then repress in analyses of the masculinism of liberal political philosophy are actually crucial. The undecidability of women in liberalism between inclusion as the subjects of universal principles applicable in the public sphere and exclusion from those universal principles as women whose proper place is in the private domestic sphere, far from being negligible, is actually constitutive of the difference between them.

Hegemony

Finally in this section, we turn to the question of the relation between political philosophy and social and political practices. This question is rarely addressed in the feminist literature on liberalism, though it seems that some kind of relation is often supposed. Where the question has been explicitly addressed, three main alternatives have been proposed.

The first is that liberalism is a reflection of socio-economic institutions, more specifically, of capitalist socio-economic relations. In the article previously referred to, Teresa Brennan and Carole Pateman argue that the liberal public/private distinction was established in early modernity with the rise of capitalism, and the subsequent shift of production out of the home, and of the liberal political system (Brennan and Pateman, 1979, pp. 185–6 and 192). Though Brennan and Pateman deny that political theory can simply be seen as reflecting socio-economic changes, in effect it is hard to see how else we are to understand the relation between them, given their argument that capitalist market relations required the liberal view of individuals:

> Individuals can not be seen as freely entering contracts and making exchanges with each other in the market, and as able freely to pursue their interests, unless they have come to be conceived as free and equal to each other. Furthermore, unless they are seen in this fashion, they have no need voluntarily to agree to, or consent to, government or the exercise of authority.
>
> (Brennan and Pateman, 1979, p. 184)

This view of political philosophy as the reflection of socio-economic changes is now largely discredited: it is overly deterministic and unable to explain how individual philosophers, who do not always directly share the socio-economic interests of the rising class, are able to articulate so exactly what is required by capitalism (Laslett's introduction to Locke, 1960, pp. 55–7). Furthermore, it assumes that the principles elaborated in political philosophy, and expressed in political life, are entirely without effect themselves, that they are but the epiphenomena of deeper causal forces (Skinner, 1988a, p. 107).

In her later work Pateman proposes a second view of the relation between political theory and practice. The public/private distinction of liberal political theory is best seen, she argues, as ideological: it obscures and mystifies the subordinate position of women. First, having defined the home as private, and therefore non-political, liberalism then forgets about it and treats the public sphere as if it existed entirely independently; it forgets the interdependence of the two in a way that obscures, for example, the economic dependence of women on male breadwinners. And second, the way in which political theory forgets about the home allows it to consider that all citizens are in fact the free and equal autonomous individuals of the public sphere; it allows it to forget women's subordination in the home (Pateman, 1989a, pp. 120–3).

The problems of the concept of ideology (in this sense; it may also be used simply to describe a world-view, or a set of linked beliefs) are also fairly well rehearsed. Probably the most important is that it presupposes that theorists have access to the 'truth' which other social actors do not possess, and this privileged access is extremely difficult to defend given the contentious nature of most social and political theory. The Marxist tradition from which the theory of ideology is derived has long been grappling with such problems; it seems clear that they are irresolvable within the terms of the Marxist paradigm itself and that we may now have reached a point, as Michèle Barrett argues, where there is a paradigm shift to a model which sees ideas and practices as more closely tied together in a theory of discourse (Barrett, 1991, pp. 46–7). In the context of this study, and of Pateman's view of political theory as ideological, we might want to argue that the 'forgetting' has never been complete, it has only ever been partial and temporary. While it is now relatively uncontroversial to argue that political theorists have 'forgotten' women in the private sphere, the same is not true of social and political movements which have attempted, throughout modernity, to institute, maintain or subvert the opposition between public and private.

The third view of the relation between political philosophy and social and political practices is that it is psychological. Political theory is produced by men and because men are socially positioned differently from women they are also psychologically different; political philosophy is always written, then, from a male perspective. As Christine DiStefano puts it:

> There is good reason to suppose that a specifically masculine cognitive orientation inhabits the terrain of modern political theory and enjoys a wide-ranging, if obscure and implicit influence . . .
>
> (DiStefano, 1991, p. 55)

This claim is rarely made explicitly by feminist critics of liberalism, but it is quite often implied. We will examine it in more detail in the next chapter. Broadly speaking it is based on the psychoanalytic theory of Nancy Chodorow, which links psychology to capitalism: because men are brought up by attentive mothers and absent fathers, in order to become masculine they learn to distance themselves from personal relationships and so perform well in the impersonal, competitive public sphere of capitalism; women, on the other hand, retain their close connection with their mothers, which makes them ideally suited to caring for the family in the private domestic sphere (Chodorow, 1978).

What is generally taken to be at stake here, both by those who hold this view and those who dispute it, is the extent to which difference between the sexes should be valued – for the sake of elevating women's position in society, and for the benefit of society as a whole – or rejected – for the sake of freeing women from a conventional identity which has resulted in their second-class status. The question of whether there is actually a difference between the sexes such that liberalism could be seen as having been produced from a male perspective is not usually addressed in this context; no doubt because in general theorists tend to be sceptical about the claims of empirical studies. Nevertheless, this view of the relation between political theory and social and political institutions presupposes the truth of Chodorow's theory: it presupposes that there is a binary opposition between the sexes, that each sex has its own distinct psychology and that liberalism encodes the masculine perspective and excludes the feminine.

If, however, as deconstruction suggests, binary oppositions are ultimately impossible, if one side of the opposition is always, necessarily, open to the other because of the undecidability that makes that opposition possible, then the absolute exclusion of the feminine from the masculine can never finally be achieved. If this is the case, it is more useful to look at historically specific attempts to open up or close down the ultimately undecidable oppositions of liberalism. It is more useful to look at social and political movements that have taken liberalism as an object, or as a tool with which to change social and political institutions, rather than supposing that there is a pre-given masculine (or feminine) psychology which will manifest itself in every social product, including political philosophy.

The relation between political philosophy and social and political institutions is, then, to be thought of in terms of a theory of hegemony. The theory of hegemony developed by Ernesto Laclau and Chantal Mouffe enables us to situate the Derridean deconstruction of texts in their historical context. Liberalism is situated as a theory which, although always turning on the same set of key terms, has been used in different ways by different social and political movements in attempts to institute, maintain and disrupt social and political relations. For our purposes here, there are two crucial points that must be taken into account in a theory of hegemony. First, hegemonic articulations are always contingent: they are not the necessary outcome of socio-economic causes, nor do they conceal a class or gender structure which the theorist can uncover, nor are they the product of a pre-given psychological will. The success of a hegemonic project lies in the linking together of elements which were previously linked in other ways, or were floating free, spread across a variety of different contexts without being related one to the other. A hegemonic project attempts to articulate these floating elements in ways which will gain support from those who were previously hostile to the project. Second, hegemony is constitutive: it institutes social identities and relations in a way that does not depend on any *a priori* social rationality, nor on any objectively given social structure. If a hegemonic project is successful, the articulations it makes must be embodied in institutions which weld together a historical bloc, a hegemonic formation (Laclau and Mouffe, 1985, pp. 134–6).

According to the theory of hegemony, the undecidability of texts that Derridean deconstruction opens up requires a decision. The moment of decision is required because the failure of identity uncovered by deconstruction is unliveable on a day-to-day basis. Social life is understood precisely as the attempt to deal with the impossibility of finally fixing identity with a singular meaning, an impossibility which constantly threatens chaos. Hegemonic projects attempt to fix the self-presence of unstable categories. Without the partial fixity they achieve, there would be no social rules; social life would be impossible (Laclau and Mouffe, 1985, p. 112). What Derrida calls an 'ethico-political' decision to read or write a text in one way rather than another (Derrida, 1988, p. 116) is seen as part of an attempt to institute a particular form of social life. It is seen as one aspect of a hegemonic project and so as contingent and, at least potentially, constitutive. There are clear limits to what can be decided: undecidability is not a vague indeterminacy, it does not mean that 'anything goes', it is always 'a *determinate* oscillation between possibilities' (Derrida, 1988, p. 148) and it is necessary that there should be a decision, but there is no necessity for the decision that is actually made. The decision that is actually made is contingent; it is made out of the determinate possibilities of a text in relation to a particular hegemonic project. And it is potentially constitutive: it aims to institute new social relations, or at least to modify those already existing (Laclau, 1993, p. 283).

This is not to say that decisions must be taken once and for all. In fact, it is impossible to take a final decision on an undecidable terrain. It is a precondition of undecidability that there is no transcendental guarantee that could finally fix the meaning of identities and the alternative possibility repressed in a decision is part of the conditions of possibility of its contestability (in Derridean terms, its constitutive outside). Undecidability can never be definitively closed off (Laclau, 1990, pp. 34–5). And in practice, as we will see, feminists have often been unwilling to close down the undecidability they have so fruitfully opened up in liberalism. Historically, the feminist movement has rarely definitively decided for one side or the other of the liberal undecidability of women. Although for practical purposes it has been, and still is, necessary to make decisions on the identity of women – in order to campaign for changes in legislation, in the gendered division of labour, in cultural representations, and so on – it is not necessary that all the small decisions that have to be made should fall on one determinate possibility and not the other. As a social movement feminism has, in different historical contexts, opened up the liberal undecidability of women, and has not tried definitively to close it down.

OUTLINE OF CHAPTERS

The study charts the feminist use of the liberal undecidability of women in three historical contexts. Close deconstructive readings are made of what are taken to have been the most influential liberal texts in the history of British social and political institutions: John Locke's *Two Treatises of Government*, John Stuart Mill's *On Liberty* and *The Subjection of Women*, and William Beveridge's Report on *Social Insurance and Allied Services*. The study has not, however, restricted itself to charting actual citations of these texts, or quotations from them, in order to show their influence, as recommended by those persuaded by the arguments of Quentin Skinner that this is the only legitimate way to do intellectual history (Skinner, 1988b; Collini, 1979, pp. 7–11). This would have meant restricting it to a very limited historical context and the principal aim of the study, to chart changes in liberal practices with particular reference to the feminist influence on those practices up to and including the present day, would have been lost. On the other hand, it tries to avoid simply assuming that liberalism is dominant in contemporary social and political institutions. This seems to be the assumption of many feminist analyses of liberalism as masculinist. The problem here is that generally the liberalism that is taken to be dominant is the classical liberalism of the seventeenth century. Such an approach is ahistoric and takes no account of changes in liberal philosophy and practice. This study tries, then, to steer a middle way between the detailed work on primary historical sources that is necessary to show that the work of a particular theorist was actually influential in any particular instance, and the forcing of an ahistoric model of liberalism onto historically specific social and political institutions. It uses secondary historical texts to examine hegemonic projects which attempted to institute categories and principles which are shown to be closely related to those of specific versions of liberalism.

The study begins by outlining the feminist critiques of liberalism as masculinist which provide the starting point of the project. We shall examine the various aspects of liberalism that feminists have analysed as essentially masculine before undertaking the deconstructive, and reconstructive, readings of liberalism that form the main body of the work. These begin in chapter 3, which looks at the liberalism of Locke in early modernity, discusses the beginning of the relationship between liberalism and feminism in anti-patriarchalism and shows how the undecidability of women constitutive of the public/private opposition central to all versions of liberalism was opened up by an early feminist, Mary Astell. In chapter 4 we then look at the liberalism of John Stuart Mill, and in particular at his articulation of liberalism and democracy. The argument presented in this chapter is that the democratisation of liberalism achieved by this articulation means that there is a significant break between the liberalism of the seventeenth century and at least some of the most influential versions of liberalism in the late twentieth century. The nineteenth century also saw the first uses of the liberal undecidability of women by feminists in political campaigns aimed at instituting new forms of the social. It is argued that feminism used the undecidability of women in Mill's liberalism *against* the categories and principles of classical liberalism. In chapter 5 it is argued that in the second half of the twentieth century three different versions of liberalism are partially instituted in social and political practices: New Liberalism, Millian liberalism and neo-liberalism. Second-wave feminism has made good use of the undecidability of women in the first two versions and that this use has been influential in preventing the closure of undecidability in the third. The feminist disruption of the public/private distinction in the late twentieth century and the extension of rights into the domestic sphere mean that the way in which we must now describe liberal-democracy as a set of social and political practices and identities is very different from that put forward, explicitly and implicitly, by the feminist critiques of liberalism outlined in chapter 2.

Finally, in the concluding chapter we look at alternatives for feminism: how should we proceed given the continuing subordination of women? It is argued that liberal-democracy allows for the affirmation of women which is required for a genuine deconstruction of the hierarchical binary opposition between the sexes. At the same time, it also allows for the possibility of keeping open the constitutive undecidability of the liberal use of women that feminism has opened up in contemporary social and political practices. Sexual inequality can be, as it has been in the past, addressed by feminism within the terms of liberal-democracy.

2 The Critique of Liberalism as Masculinist

We begin, then, with the feminist critique of liberalism as masculinist. This provides the initial problem of this project; in the rest of the study we shall be assessing the extent to which liberalism can reasonably be characterised in this way. It also, however, provides the framework for a substantive model of gendered social and political institutions. Although we shall be taking issue with the *rigidity* of the model feminist critiques propose, they nevertheless provide invaluable insights into forms of social life, historical and contemporary, without which the analysis of liberalism as gendered that will be made in following chapters, different as it is in certain important respects from the model outlined in this one, would not have been possible.[1]

Feminist critiques of liberalism as masculinist must be situated in the context of what we can think of as a 'paradigm shift' in feminist theory since the beginning of its most recent productive period in the 1970s. There has been a paradigm shift in that basic assumptions have now been overturned. From approaches which, broadly speaking, took differences between men and women as the pathological foundations and expressions of patriarchy, and which generally saw them as eradicable in the name of equality and liberation, feminist theorising has shifted to taking those differences to be both more intransigent and more positive (Barrett and Phillips, 1992, p. 4). Informed by questions of political strategy this shift has also been the product of theoretical questioning of the crucial distinction on which this androgynous vision was based: the sex/gender distinction.

POSTMODERN AND DIFFERENCE FEMINISM

The sex/gender distinction posits an arbitrary connection between the male body and masculinity and the female body and femininity which is historically specific and therefore open to radical change. As Ann Oakley put it in 1972:

That people are male or female can usually be judged by referring to the biological evidence. That they are masculine or feminine cannot be judged in the same way: the criteria are cultural, differing with time and place. The constancy of sex must be admitted, but so also must the variability of gender

(Oakley, 1985, p. 16)

The critique of the sex/gender distinction takes two main forms in the contemporary debate between feminists: that of what we can loosely call postmodern feminism and that of 'difference' feminism. Both begin from a similar difficulty: the sex/gender distinction presupposes an unwarranted split between biology and society, between the neutrally given body which is discovered in science and the socially constructed consciousness of gender. From this point they take divergent paths.

From a postmodern perspective Judith Butler argues that sex itself is a gendered category. Along Foucauldian lines she sees sex as produced in discourse: gender should not be thought of as the meaning which is attached to pre-given sex; rather the scientific discourse in which sex is 'discovered' is itself a gendered apparatus of production. As she puts it:

gender is not to culture as sex is to nature; gender is also the discursive/cultural means by which 'sexed nature' or 'a natural sex' is produced and established as 'pre-discursive', prior to culture, a politically neutral surface on which culture acts.

(Butler, 1990, p. 7)

Although Butler argues that we cannot step outside the cultural meanings in which sex is produced, it would seem on her account that both sex and gender are, in principle at least, infinitely malleable. In response to a question from Lynne Segal charging her with neglecting biological constraints on bodies', Butler replies:

I do not deny certain kinds of biological differences. But I always ask under what conditions, under what discursive and institutional conditions, do certain biological differences – and they're not necessary ones, given the anomalous state of bodies in the world – become the salient characteristics of sex.

(Butler, 1994, pp. 33–4)

Her answer is confused because on her theoretical arguments it is only 'under certain discursive and institutional conditions' that we can speak of or recognise biological differences at all; biological differences are themselves produced in discursive practices. There are *discursive* constraints on the construction of the sexed body, but it is meaningless on Butler's theory to think of biological differences as producing extra-discursive constraints in the way Segal is suggesting. And insofar as constraints are discursive it is impossible to specify *a priori* the extent to which they limit the construction of the body in different forms. This is in contrast to 'difference' feminists. In fact, according to Butler, insofar as feminism posits 'women' as an identity, as 'difference' feminists do, it contributes to the binary categorisation of sex that sustains what she calls the 'heterosexual matrix' – the assumption that sex, gender and sexuality are dichotomous unities – and the masculinist hegemony and heterosexist power that are supported by it (Butler, 1990, p. 5). In this respect feminism contributes to the discursive constraints that are productive of the heterosexual body. What feminism should do, according to Butler, is to look for dissonances in this matrix by calling attention to occasions on which what are taken to be attributes of one gender are enacted by members of what are taken to be the other; in the subversive repetition of heterosexual relations that 'butch' and 'femme' lesbians enact, for example (p. 31). In this way the binary opposition of the heterosexual matrix will be displaced by a proliferation of identities from within its terms.

Butler and 'difference' feminists agree that the aim of the feminist project should be to undermine masculine hegemony and heterosexist power, but they disagree on how to proceed. From the difference perspective it is argued that even if the body is constructed and not given in the discourses in which it is an object, 'The present and future enhancement of the powers and capacities of women must take account of the ways in which their bodies are presently constituted' (Gatens, 1992, p. 133). On this view the sexed body insists on being recognised and the historically specific meanings associated with the physical differences between male and female bodies cannot be ignored. At the most obvious level, as Jessie Barnard puts it, 'Men hardly ever get pregnant!' (Bacchi, 1990, p. x) The body intervenes to confirm or deny social significances that are attached to it and this ties femininity and femaleness and masculinity and maleness much more closely than either the sex/gender distinction, or the postmodern perspective, allows (Gatens, 1991a, p. 146). As Gatens puts it:

> the relation between masculine behaviour acted out by a male subject and masculine behaviour acted out by a female subject (or feminine

behaviour acted out by a female subject and feminine behaviour acted out by a male subject) cannot be symmetrical.

(p. 150)

As Gatens points out, taking these relations as historically contingent but not arbitrary need not imply biological reductionism since the point is to investigate the social significance of the sexed body and its associations with 'femininity', 'women', 'masculinity' and 'men' (p. 149). But it does seem to imply that there are important limits to the extent to which differences between the sexes can be ignored or transformed.

It is from this perspective that the feminist critiques of liberalism as masculinist have been developed. These approaches begin from the premise that there are physical differences between the sexes that cannot be ignored. According to Carole Pateman, for example, an adequate political theory must take into account that women have a capacity that men do not have: that of giving birth (Pateman, 1986, p. 7). From this premise feminists then go on to argue two different points which neither imply, nor exclude, each other but which are not clearly distinguished in the literature. First, that in masculinist political theory women and men are associated with different capacities and attributes and with different areas of society. And second, that women and men actually have or enact different capacities and attributes and have actually been positioned in different areas of society. Before we look into this confusion we shall look at two theories that have been extremely influential in difference feminism; both possibilities are based on these theories and to some extent the confusion between them is already featured there.

The first theory is elaborated in Nancy Chodorow's *The Reproduction of Mothering*. She argues that from the sexed difference in infants follow differences in the ways in which women and men relate to others. Chodorow adopts an object-relations approach in psychoanalytic theory which puts the emphasis in infantile development on the desire to attain and maintain relationships with others, rather than on the drives and unconscious phantasies of the individual as it develops. In this respect, she argues, object-relations theory is different from Freudian psychoanalytic theory (Chodorow, 1978, pp. 45–52). I do not intend to go into this question here, but only to point out that for Chodorow infantile development is grounded in ongoing social practices and it is the way in which parents – especially mothers – relate to children as always already sexed that explains the reproduction of masculinity and femininity in her work.[2] Chodorow's question is, why do women mother in the way they do in the conventional nuclear families of contemporary Western society? Or rather, why do they want to mother in this way and get a good deal of satisfaction from doing so? For her the answer lies in the different experiences of the sexes in relation to their own mothers and in particular to their desire to separate from them. According to Chodorow, the infant's early relationship with his/her mother is experienced as one of fusion, a merging which is associated with complete satisfaction but which is also threatening to the emerging sense of self as a distinct being (pp. 78–83). As a result of this threat, infants of both sexes try to distance themselves from the mother, while at the same time they continue to want to possess her for themselves (pp. 96–7). For the girl this is more problematic, according to Chodorow, because while the mother distinguishes the boy child as different from herself and encourages this difference, she is inclined to identify with the daughter and to continue to see her as an extension of herself (p. 109). Although girls do turn from the mother towards the father in the Oedipus complex on Chodorow's account, they do not thereby reject her as inferior, as Freud had it, because of her lack of penis. Rather they are ambivalent towards her, attempting to separate from her by possessing the penis – a symbol of differentiation from the mother – and also trying to win her love at the same time – it is clear to them that she prefers people with penises (p. 125). According to Chodorow, girls do not give up the initial infantile sense of oneness with the mother completely in the way that boys do; they retain this early sense of connectedness with her and it is this that women are trying to reproduce in their own desire to mother. Furthermore, as a result of their continuing sense of relatedness with their own mothers they have the capacities that are necessary to mother a young child; they have the ability to empathise with the child and to take responsibility for his/her needs in a selfless way (p. 204). Boys, on the other hand, have to repress their early identification with the mother in order to separate from her and to identify with the father. Since in modern Western families men are largely absent, the identification boys make with the father is tenuous, Chodorow suggests; it is an identification with the *position* of the father as a man, rather than the result of an emotional relationship as was the early sense of oneness with the mother (pp. 175–6). As a result men's sense of masculinity is fragile, according to Chodorow, and they have continually to deny and repress whatever they take to be feminine in order to identify themselves as male. They have a stronger sense of autonomy than women, but this is at the expense of their ability to relate to others affectively (p. 181).

I do not want to go into criticisms of Chodorow's theory here; our object is to discuss its influence on political theory and there is no doubt that it has been influential, whatever its problems.[3] This influence has been partly mediated through the work of Carol Gilligan, which draws on Chodorow's work to make the case that men and women use different criteria in order to arrive at moral decisions. At least, that is Gilligan's initial argument, and this is how her work has been used by many difference feminists. In fact, however, Gilligan's position is not so straightforward.

In a Different Voice, Gilligan's (1982) most influential work, argues that there are two very different ways of reasoning morally. The first – the ethic of justice – is concerned to judge what should be done in the light of universal principles which would hold for any situation. It attributes rights to individuals which can be ranked hierarchically in accordance with reason such that any rational being would arrive at the same decision in a moral dilemma. In contrast to this approach is the ethic of care which sees moral judgements much more tentatively as specific to particular individuals in particular situations which can not be universalised. It sees individuals in a much more concrete way as having characteristics peculiar to them and especially focuses on the relationships between people in the situation in which a moral decision has to be taken; it is on the basis of individual characteristics and personal relationships that a judgement is considered right. Such an approach – sensitive to the details of situations and reluctant to make moral judgements – may also be termed 'contextual relativism' (Friedman, 1987b, p. 191). The principal difference between the ethics of care and the ethics of justice, however, lies in the relationship that is assumed or envisaged between self and other. As Kittay and Meyers put it in their introduction to *Women and Moral Theory*:

> A morality of rights and abstract reason begins with a moral agent who is separate from others, and who independently elects moral principles to obey. In contrast, a morality of responsibility and care begins with a self who is enmeshed in a network of relations to others, and whose moral deliberation aims to maintain these relations.
>
> (Kittay and Meyers, 1987, p. 10)

The relation between Gilligan's work and Chodorow's is immediately apparent: both distinguish between the feminine self-in-relation to the other and the masculine self-as-detached from the other. In fact, Gilligan draws on Chodorow's model of infantile development, arguing that it better explains the differences between the development of boys and girls than does Freud's (Gilligan, 1982, pp. 6–9). Repeatedly, throughout *In a Different Voice* women are described as defining themselves through attachment to others, while men are described as detached, and afraid of that attachment. However, Gilligan is not clear about the relationship between femininity and the 'different voice' she has discovered. Although in *In a Different Voice* she argues that the association she has made between women and the ethics of care is an empirical one, she notes that it is not absolute and that generalisations about the sexes should not be made on the basis of this piece of work (p. 2). Nevertheless, this disclaimer is not enough to counteract the repeated association between men and the voice of detached principles and women and the voice of attached care that predominates in the book.[4] The associations Gilligan makes between femininity and the ethics of care and masculinity and the ethics of justice and the ways in which these have been taken up in the feminist critiques of liberalism as masculinist are ambiguous.

Both Chodorow's and Gilligan's theories are used in two different ways which, as I stated earlier, are not always clearly distinguished. The first is to accept Chodorow's conclusion that there is a substantive difference between men and women in terms of their relations to others. From this perspective Christine DiStefano argues that male political theorists have produced an account of modernity which attempts to repress and deny the feminine and to assert a clearly demarcated and autonomous masculine individual. Some of the elements of this masculine world view are, according to DiStefano:

> a combative brand of dualistic thinking, a persistent and systematic amplification of the primal self–other oppositional dynamic and the creation of dichotomously structured polarities with which to describe the events, objects and processes of the natural and social worlds. . . . The explicit or implicit denial of relatedness – to 'fellow' human beings, to women, and to nature. . . . attitudes of fear, denigration, and hostility toward whatever is identified as female or feminine, along with its idealization and glorification. Both sets of seemingly incompatible attitudes recapitulate the effects of false differentiation from, of unsuccessful rapprochement with, the maternal subject-object.
> (DiStefano, 1991, pp. 60–1)

The editors of *Ethics: A Feminist Reader* are also clear that there are actually substantive differences between the subjectivity of women and men in this respect. They see the categories and oppositions of political theory as related to the way in which masculine and feminine subjectivity has actually been differently constructed in social institutions. Women in modern Europe, they argue, have been taught to be feminine – to be considerate of others and aware of their vulnerability – in a way that is directly linked to what is seen as their biological function of bearing and raising children, while the masculinity of men – involving a sense of personal importance and the need to make one's way in the world of work and politics on the basis of the development of one's autonomous capacities – is supported by a range of social institutions which generate a sense of self, at least partly, by excluding women as the 'Other'. Frazer et al. see liberalism as encoding this specifically masculine subjectivity:

the important point about this distinctively 'feminine' character-structure is its incompatibility with the image of the untrammelled, self-determining subject so familiar from moral and political philosophy. What the feminist critique of ethics has helped us to see is that if the salient features of your social experience are seeking to please, fitting in with others, being the one whom others count on . . . then it is no cause for surprise if you regard that familiar image either as irrelevant or as a cue for feelings of inadequacy.

(Frazer et al., 1992, p. 6)

Similarly, Seyla Benhabib takes Gilligan to have shown that 'Women's moral development is more contextual, more immersed in the details of relationships and narratives. Women show a greater propensity to take the standpoint of the "particular other" and appear more adept at revealing feelings of empathy and sympathy required by this' (Benhabib, 1987, p. 155). As a result, she argues, contractarian political theories, from Hobbes to Rawls, in which the ideal of moral autonomy is defined in terms of universalist principles have meant the privatisation of women's experience and its exclusion from a moral point of view (p. 158).

Other feminist critics of liberalism as masculinist are much less explicit than DiStefano, Frazer et al. and Benhabib about their commitment to an *actual* difference between the sexes along the lines of Chodorow's and Gilligan's theories. The feminist critic of liberalism as masculinist whose work has probably been most influential in the field, Carole Pateman, generally writes as if the associations she details in modern political theory between women and care for particular others in the private sphere as opposed to men and principles of abstract justice in the public sphere are important at the level of theory only. She writes that:

> investigations have been uncovering how the understanding of ['male-stream'] theory is dependent on an opposition to women and all that is symbolised by the feminine and women's bodies, and why traditionally, women's intuition and deficiency in rationality have been presented as the antithesis of the logic, order and reason required of theorists.
>
> (Pateman, 1986, p. 3)

From this perspective we might be inclined to see Chodorow's and Gilligan's work as contributing to the *problem* of the association between these terms, as reiterating them, rather than as offering a challenge to mainstream political theory. It is difficult to draw this conclusion from Pateman's work, however. She never discusses Chodorow's or Gilligan's work or considers the relation between theoretical categories and oppositions and the possibility that women and men may *actually* relate differently to others, but her theoretical position does seem to presuppose that there is a substantive difference between the two sexes in this respect. She suggests that modern political theory is best seen as a 'defence of masculinity against the dangers of femininity' (Pateman, 1986, p. 2). The point here would seem to be that it is because modern political theory has been written by *men*, with a particular need to define themselves as masculine against the feminine, that it adopts its traditional concepts, categories and oppositions. Furthermore, she states that her object in uncovering the masculinity of modern political theory is to illuminate the patriarchal structure of contemporary society:

> My interest in the sexual contract is not primarily in interpreting texts, although the classic works of social contract theory figure largely in my discussion. I am resurrecting the story in order to throw light onto the present structure of major social institutions in Britain, Australia and the United States – societies which, we are told, can properly be seen as if they originated in a social contract. The sense in which these societies are patriarchal can be elucidated through the full story of the original contract . . .
>
> (Pateman, 1988, p. 4)

This does not necessarily mean that men and women are masculine and feminine in Chodorow's or Gilligan's sense, but it does imply a close connection between political theory and political and social practices which, as noted in the previous chapter, is not adequately theorised in Pateman's work. Because Pateman suggests this close connection, because she tends to treat liberalism as if it were a kind of empirical theory, albeit somewhat distorted, of actual social and political institutions, her work lends itself well to comparison with the way in which liberalism is treated in this study. It is similar to Pateman's work in that it also takes liberalism to be more than simply political philosophy. But it differs in its methodology: reading texts deconstructively it does not reify binary oppositions as Pateman's readings do and, using the theory of hegemony, it situates those texts more precisely in their historical context. As a result, it also differs in its conclusions. It is because Pateman aims, however, to treat liberalism as if it were in some way constitutive of social and political institutions that her work will be important in subsequent chapters as a point of comparison with the understanding of liberalism that is being developed here.

THE MASCULINE INDIVIDUAL

Apart from the view that there is a fundamental and ineradicable difference between the sexes, and following on from this point, the theme that unites the feminist critique of liberalism as masculinist that will be examined in the following chapters is that its central categories are only ostensibly universal; in fact they are proper only to masculine capacities, attributes and activities (Pateman, 1986; Young, 1990; Gatens, 1991a; Cavarero, 1992; Phillips, 1992). It is important to distinguish between three different senses of 'masculine' in this context. First, it is used in the sense detailed by Chodorow and Gilligan as detached, judging according to rational universal principles, and so on. Second, it may refer to differences in the way the sexes have been historically positioned – as mothers or as breadwinners, for example – a position which may be agnostic concerning differences in the actual subjectivities of women and men. And third, it may also mean 'masculine' by association with the categories 'man' or 'men' within the theory itself, a position which, as we have seen in the case of the work of Carole Pateman, is ambiguous about this difference. The most important liberal category theorised as masculinist is that of the individual.

The individual of liberalism is held to be masculine in all three senses outlined above. In the first sense, Seyla Benhabib argues that the state of nature of classical contract theorists provides a vision of the individual as an autonomous self that is the dream (Rousseau) and also the nightmare (Hobbes) of the bourgeois male. It is Hobbes, she says, who gives this dream its clearest formulation: 'Let us consider men . . . as if even now sprung out of the earth, and suddenly, like mushrooms, come to full maturity, without all kind of engagement to each other' (quoted in Benhabib, 1987, p. 161). For Benhabib this metaphor expresses the ultimate vision of autonomy: the mother of whom every individual is born disappears and is replaced by the earth, releasing the male ego from any dependence on another (p. 161). Along similar lines DiStefano makes a detailed analysis of Mill's *On Liberty*, in which she compares the self-sufficient and sovereign individual who requires a 'protected zone of thought, expression and action for his survival and well-being' with which the book is concerned with the subject of Gilligan's 'different voice'. DiStefano argues that from the point of view of this feminine subject, for whom a sense of connection and ongoing responsibility for others is so important, the rights of the individual to non-interference make little sense (p. 172).

Linked to this approach is the argument that the individual of liberal theory is masculine because it performs roles and takes part in activities that historically have only been available to men. As feminists repeatedly point out, the individual of modern political theory is invariably a head of household, traditionally a position that only men have held. Moira Gatens argues along these lines that John Stuart Mill has taken what men do as the norm from which he has constructed his notion of the individual. According to Gatens he fails to address women's work in the domestic sphere *as* work because in the liberal tradition in which he is situated work is entered into by means of contracts between free and equal individuals. This is a theory of work in terms of a wage-relation which cannot be applied to women's work in the home, since care for others is not easily quantified, and so Mill is not able to theorise it as social or cultural; he is compelled to see it simply as the natural precondition of wage-labour outside the home (Gatens, 1992, pp. 34–9). To be an individual on Mill's scheme, Gatens argues, women must work outside the home in the market but, although Mill allows for women to make this choice as individuals, if they should all choose to do so it is impossible to see how society could be reproduced (p. 46). In other words, on Mill's scheme women cannot be the free and equal individuals of liberalism because the wage-relations into which those individuals enter in the market depend on their unpaid labour in the home. On Mill's theory the individual can only be the male head of household. Along similar lines Annette Baier argues that the liberal vision of society as made up of detached, rational individuals is not well able to describe the work in which women are most often involved. It does not well suit the assumption of parental responsibility, for example, which involves an ongoing relation of care and love in which the justice of controlling reason plays at best an equal role with the cultivation of desirable emotions (Baier, 1987). In this case, the liberal individual is seen to be masculine by default; it cannot easily be fitted to a description of mothering, probably the paradigm case of a feminine activity in modern Western societies.

Finally, there are arguments which see the individual as masculine because of the way it is explicitly associated with the attributes and roles of men and opposed to those of women within the work of the political theorist himself. In this respect it can be seen, as I pointed out earlier, as indicative of a substantive difference in subjectivity between the sexes – as 'a defence of the masculine against the dangers of the feminine' – even where the question of the relation between the theory and actual social practices is not addressed. On this account the masculinity of the individual is ensured by the way in which its capacities, attributes and activities are defined as *not* female. At the most obvious level Carole Pateman simply states that for classical liberal theorists, 'Men alone have the attributes of free and equal "individuals".... Women are born into subjection' (Pateman, 1988, p. 41). But, more importantly, it is not possible simply to recategorise women under the generic term 'man', so allowing them equal rights with men; the individual is masculine precisely because women, in their embodied difference from men and because of the meanings that are associated with that difference, are not, and can not be, liberal individuals. As Pateman puts it:

> The masculine, public world, the universal world of individualism, rights, contract, reason, freedom, equality, impartial law and citizenship . . . gains its meaning and significance only in contrast with and in opposition to, the private world of particularity, natural subjection, inequality, emotion, love, partiality – and women and femininity . . .
>
> (Pateman, 1986, p. 6)

Women cannot be the free and equal individuals of liberalism because of their position in the private sphere and their association with values *opposed* to the public sphere in which liberal individuals have their place.

THE PUBLIC/PRIVATE OPPOSITION

Crucial from the perspective of feminist critiques of liberalism, then, is the opposition it makes between public and private spheres. From the feminist point of view the individual of liberal theory is autonomous and able to reason according to universal, rational principles only because the emotional and physical interdependence of embodied individuals is excluded from the public sphere in which he is situated. It is relegated to the private domestic sphere where women, who have the capacities to care for others and lack those required to participate in the public sphere, are naturally subject to men. As Seyla Benhabib puts it:

> The sphere of justice, from Hobbes, through Locke and Kant, is regarded as the domain wherein independent, male heads-of-household transact with one another, while the domestic-intimate sphere is put beyond the pale of justice and restricted to the reproductive and affective needs of the bourgeois *paterfamilias*. . . . An entire domain of human activity, namely nurture, reproduction, love and care, which becomes the woman's lot in the course of the development of modern bourgeois society, is excluded from moral and political considerations, and confined to the realm of 'nature'.
>
> (Benhabib, 1987, p. 160)

The masculine individual in the public sphere is actually, then, unlike any concrete individual, disembodied. Every individual in the public sphere is alike, each may be substituted for the other since they are all subject to universal rational principles which do not distinguish between them. In Benhabib's terms, individuals in the public sphere take the place of the 'generalised other', they have no characteristics peculiar to themselves as individuals that would interfere with the universality of the laws which they make and which they agree to live by (p. 163). Sexual difference, like all the other differences of concrete individuals, is excluded from the public sphere and features only in the private sphere of love and care (p. 162; see also Young, 1990).

On the liberal model, then, there are no individuals in the private feminine sphere of love and care. The universal principles of equality and freedom that apply in the public sphere have no place there. This means that the domestic sphere in which women are subordinate to men is seen as outside the liberal realm of politics and outside the scope of the law (Phillips, 1987a, pp. 12–13). In *Sexual Divisions in*

Law Katherine O'Donovan describes how the law and legal theory derived from liberalism have contributed to the construction of public and private as two separate spheres regulated by opposing sets of values. The private domestic sphere has been associated with the *Gemeinschaft* values of status, love, duty and common understanding in contrast to the *Gesellschaft* values of the public sphere in which individuals are seen as competing for advantage and which is regulated by formal contract, neutrality of adjudication, rationality and predictability. According to O'Donovan, women, who are seen in law primarily in the context of reproduction, home and family, are positioned as the guardians of the values of *Gemeinschaft*, the private domestic sphere is seen as ordered according to an ideology of love and is therefore thought to be unsuitable for legal regulation (O'Donovan, 1985, pp. 11–12). As the authors of the foreword to a text on legal theory put it in 1970:

> The normal behaviour of husband and wife or parents and children towards each other is beyond the law – as long as the family is 'healthy'. The law comes in when things go wrong. More than that, the mere hint by anyone concerned that the law may come in is the surest sign that things are or will soon be going wrong.
>
> (O. Kahn-Freund and K.W. Wedderburn,
> quoted in O'Donovan, 1985, p. 13)

As feminists have long pointed out, what this means is that the power of men over women in the domestic sphere is thereby supported, both by the way in which particular family forms are actually structured by state regulation, and by the way the state fails to intervene to protect or support women gainst men in the home (O'Donovan, 1985, pp. 14–15; Phillips, 1987a, p. 13). Liberalism constructs an opposition between public and private that has naturalised women's subordination and refused them the ostensibly universal status of free and equal individual.

Furthermore, the feminist critique of liberalism as masculinist maintains that women cannot be free and equal individuals in the public sphere either. They can achieve this status only insofar as they are able to approximate the liberal individual's disembodiment. On the feminist account, legislation and institutions in the public sphere accord with liberal principles only insofar as they are gender-neutral. In Benhabib's terms, individuals must be 'generalised others', interchangeable one for the other in laws of universal scope, and the fact of their embodiment in two different sexes must be ignored as irrelevant. Up to a point, feminists argue, the disembodiment of the liberal individual has meant that liberalism has been used productively; it has meant that liberalism has been useful as a way of challenging sex discrimination and women's exclusion from formal equality with men. However, it is also argued that the very usefulness of liberalism in this respect is its limitation. On the liberal model, liberty and equality for women in the public sphere is only achieved by *decategorising* gender, by proscribing the use of sex as a basis of legal and political practices, and this leads to the neglect of substantive inequalities between the sexes which persist in the face of formal equalities (Frazer and Lacey, 1993, pp. 78–80). An example of the problems that arise for women from the liberal privileging of gender-neutrality is the application of anti-discrimination legislation to pregnant employees in the UK: at different times it has been ruled that discrimination against pregnant women is not really discrimination because it does not favour similarly situated *men*; at other times that it may constitute discrimination in comparison with the treatment that would have been accorded a sick or disabled man (pp. 81–2). In other words, the specificity of women's embodiment cannot be recognised in liberalism as a result of its commitment to the abstract disembodied individual as the bearer of universal rights. In fact, what this example shows is that it is actually the male body that has been encoded in liberalism such that, on the feminist account, liberal principles can never simply be extended to women.

Finally, and somewhat paradoxically perhaps, it is argued by feminists that when women are incorporated into the public sphere of liberalism it is specifically *as* women. According to Pateman women are accepted in the public sphere only as members of the private sphere, as dependants concerned with the unpaid care of others, who therefore cannot be equal with other (male) citizens (Pateman, 1989a). On the face of it this seems an odd claim since it might seem that the main point of the feminist critique of liberalism is that for women to be equal with men their distinctive capacities and position in the private sphere must be recognised. But Pateman's argument is that so long as male attributes and activities are the norm, where women's specificity is recognised, as it is in the welfare state, they can only be seen in inferior terms. Pateman calls this 'Wollstonecraft's dilemma':

On the one hand [women] have demanded that the ideal of citizenship be extended to them, and the liberal-feminist agenda for a 'gender-neutral' social world is the logical conclusion of one form of this demand. On the other hand, women have also insisted, often simultaneously, as did Mary Wollstonecraft, that *as women* they have specific capacities, talents, needs and concerns, so that the expression of their citizenship will be differentiated from that of men.

(p. 197)

According to Pateman, the problem is that these two demands are incompatible because the patriarchal understanding of citizenship, in which men are taken as the norm, allows two alternatives only: either 'women become (like) men, and so full citizens', something they cannot do; they can only ever be lesser men. Or 'they continue women's work, which is of no value for citizenship' (p. 197). Women *as* women can no more be free and equal with men than they can by denying their gender; in order for women to achieve citizenship as autonomous, equal and yet sexually different beings from men, the ideals of citizenship themselves have to change (Pateman, 1988, p. 14).

Feminist critics of liberalism as masculinist present, then, a convincing reading of liberal political theory as inflected with a male bias such that it must necessarily be exclusionary of women's claims to citizenship and subversive of feminist bids for equality and freedom. On this reading liberalism is *essentially* masculinist; it could not be otherwise without ceasing to be liberalism. It is this essentialist view of liberalism that I want to take issue with in this study. I will suggest that although it has contributed to women's subordination in the private sphere, liberalism is not as monolithic nor as historically uniform as the feminist critique suggests.

3 Ambivalent Anti-patriarchalism

In this chapter we shall follow Carole Pateman in looking back to early modernity as the period in which the masculinity of the liberal individual, and the public/private opposition which sustains it, were established in theory and in practice. According to Pateman, the masculinity of liberal categories and principles was made explicit in early liberal texts; political theorists had no compunction about excluding women from the universal principles of the public sphere and confining them to the private. As the tradition developed, she suggests, liberals became more coy about sexual difference; women were forgotten and eventually it came to be assumed that they were, or should be, included in universal principles of liberty and equality:

> Commentaries on the texts gloss over the fact that the classical theorists construct a patriarchal account of masculinity and femininity, of what it is to be men and women. Only masculine beings are endowed with the attributes and capacities necessary to enter into contracts . . . only men, that is to say, are individuals.
>
> (Pateman, 1988, pp. 5–6)

Until recently editors frequently removed embarrassing passages dealing with women's characteristics from the great works. In the case of Locke, prior to the feminist re-appropriation of canonical texts, the *First Treatise on Government* which is very much concerned with women's position in relation to their husbands, was considered only of historical interest and, in comparison with the *Second Treatise*, was very little read (Coole, 1988, p. 85). 'Man' was taken to be the norm and the differences political philosophers made between the sexes were taken to be an irrelevant product of an unenlightened historical period; actually women are just like men.

According to Pateman, then, it is important to recover the history of women's position in liberalism in order to understand how, far from being actually gender-neutral, its categories and principles were founded on a patriarchal construction of sexual difference. They were founded on the exclusion and subordination of women. Pateman's thesis is that liberalism today, and political theory more generally, is still constructed along much the same lines as in early modernity; it is simply that its masculinity has become obscured, it has taken on the guise of neutrality (Pateman, 1989b, p. 123).

Furthermore, insofar as Pateman is concerned to recover the history of the construction of sexual difference in liberalism in order to shed light on women's position in contemporary society, the implication is that social and political institutions have also remained much the same, at least as far as the liberal opposition between public and private and women's position in relation to it is concerned. As she puts it:

> Today, despite a large measure of civil equality, it appears natural that wives are subordinate just because they are dependent on their husbands for subsistence, and it is taken for granted that liberal social life can be understood without reference to the [private] sphere of subordination, natural relations and women.
>
> (Pateman, 1989b, p. 123)

Of course, as Pateman notes, the public/private opposition is not identical in contemporary society to that theorised by Locke; on the contrary, there is a great deal of confusion about where the distinction should be made (p. 122). Most importantly, the distinction between the private domestic sphere and civil society and the state as public is no longer the only version as it was for Locke. In advanced capitalist societies liberalism may oppose the economic sphere as private to the state-funded public sector, or civil society as private to the public sphere of the state. In both these versions, however, the domestic sphere is overlooked. In fact, Pateman argues, these other versions of the public/private opposition have contributed to obscuring the gendered distinction which is made between the home and the rest of society, and which she is concerned to recover in theory and practice (p. 122). We shall, then, follow Pateman in tracing the beginning of this gendered separation between public and private to the liberal texts of early modernity, in order to retrieve the 'forgotten' exclusion of women from the public sphere of universal liberal principles.

In this chapter we shall discuss John Locke's *Two Treatises of Government*, a text which provides, according to Pateman, '[t]he theoretical basis for the liberal separation of the public and the private' (Pateman, 1989b, p. 120).[1] Her reading of Locke offers important insights into the relation between women's subordination and liberalism but I will take issue with the way in which she represses the ambiguities of Locke's

text. Although in principle Pateman argues that 'Women's political
position . . . is full of paradoxes, ironies and contradictions' (Pateman,
1989, p. 4), in practice her reading of Locke represses the ambiguity
in his positioning of women in relation to the distinction between public and private, political and non-political. Locke is highly inconsistent in his treatment of women, seeing them sometimes as the same as
men, with the same capacities and the same relation to political society, while at other times he sees them as different from men, naturally subordinate to them and excluded from the public sphere of politics.
It is this ambiguity that a Derridean deconstructive reading of Locke's
text will show to be vitally constitutive of the public/private opposition itself.

PATEMAN'S READING OF LOCKE'S *TWO TREATISES*

In theory, Pateman argues, liberalism stands unequivocally opposed to
patriarchalism. Liberalism is based on individualism, egalitarianism and
conventionalism, while patriarchalism claims that hierarchical relations
of subordination are based on natural differences. Where Locke's ad-
versary, Sir Robert Filmer, saw political power as guaranteed by the
ruler's descent from Adam and by his fatherly relation to his people,
Locke argued that political power was conventional and that, because
all individuals are born free and equal, rule is only just if it is consented to. Political power is not the same as paternal power, as Filmer
had claimed; only the latter is based on a natural relationship, it is confined to the domestic sphere and ends with the maturity of the children. However, Pateman points out, what commentators generally fail
to notice is that Locke's separation of the familial and the political is
also a division between the sexes. Locke assumes that there must be a
sole source of authority in the household and that it would naturally
fall to the man, as 'the abler and stronger', to exercise that authority
(Pateman, 1989b, pp. 120–1).

In an early article written with Teresa Brennan, Pateman argues that
in some respects Locke seems to consider women as free and equal
individuals in the way that men are, he seems to offer them the same
possibilities of political power that men were to enjoy in political society. Locke argues against equating husbands' power over wives with
the political power of monarchs over subjects, and, on some occasions
at least, he also argues against seeing it as natural. He states that husbands' power over wives is contractual, that husbands have no right to

exercise the ultimate political power of life or death over wives, that women have equal rights over their children which husbands cannot interfere with, and even that women have the right to own property by virtue of their labour (Brennan and Pateman, 1979, p. 192). Brennan and Pateman see this, however, as the least important side of Locke's argument concerning the status of women. Although he sees husbands' power over wives as contractual, he assumes that a free and equal female individual will always enter into a marriage contract that places her in subjection to her husband. And in fact, he goes so far as to argue that though husbands' power over wives is contractual, and therefore conventional, it does have 'a Foundation in nature' (pp. 192–3). Since a natural subordinate cannot at the same time be free and equal, Pateman concludes, women are excluded from the status of 'individuals' and so from participating in the public world of equality, consent and convention (Pateman, 1989b, p. 121).

Pateman recognises, then, that there are ambiguities and even outright contradictions concerning women in Locke's text but ultimately she concludes that these are insignificant. Liberalism opened up possibilities for women that were not fulfilled because of the patriarchal development of capitalism. In early modernity the separation between the home and the means of production, which was to be so crucial to modern forms of women's oppression, began; the household lost its pre-eminence as the site of production as waged labour outside the home became increasingly the norm (Brennan and Pateman, 1979, pp. 185–7). Locke's liberalism repeats or mirrors capitalist socio-economic relations in theory by positioning women as subordinate in the private sphere and excluding them from the public sphere of individual rights. And for liberal-capitalism, Pateman argues, the separation between home and work, between public and private, is not simply a matter of practical expediency; as we can clearly see in the *Second Treatise* it is overlaid with a significance which reaches beyond the merely practical. Pateman argues that women's status in the *Second Treatise* is *exemplary* of the principles of the private sphere as opposed to those of the public:

> Locke's theory ... shows how the private and public are grounded in opposing principles of association which are exemplified in the conflicting status of women and men; natural subordination stands opposed to free individualism. The family is based on natural ties of sentiment and blood and on the sexually ascribed status of wife and husband, (mother and father). Participation in the public sphere is

governed by universal, impersonal and conventional criteria of achieve-
ment, interests, rights, equality and property – liberal criteria applicable only to men.

(Pateman, 1989b, p. 121)

And at the root of this opposition between public and private, political
and non-political is, she suggests, the most fundamental of all oppositions, that between men and women:

> In popular (and academic) consciousness the duality of female and
> male often serves to encapsulate or represent the series (or circle)
> of liberal separations and oppositions: female, or – nature, personal,
> emotional, love, private, intuition, morality, ascription, particular, sub-
> jection; male, or – culture, political, reason, justice, public, philos-
> ophy, power, achievement, universal, freedom.

(pp. 123–4)

Pateman sees Locke, then, as constructing a binary opposition between the public sphere of men and masculine principles and values
on the one hand, and the private sphere of women and feminine values
on the other. In order to read the text in this way, however, she has
had to suppress the ambiguities and contradictions that she initially
identified in Locke's text, and to regard them as irrelevant. Arguably,
she has to repress in Locke's text what has been and may be most
useful to feminism in liberalism in order to produce a reading of liberal political philosophy as oppressive to women. Using the method of
Derridean deconstruction outlined in chapter 1, I want to propose a
reading of Locke which enables both the oppressive aspects and the
emancipatory aspects of liberalism to be explored.

LOCKE'S *TWO TREATISES* AND THE UNDECIDABILITY OF 'WOMEN'

The Derridean identification of undecidability, and more specifically
of the hymen, will enable us to understand how 'woman' operates in
the *Two Treatises*. It will enable us to see how the inconsistencies of
Locke's text – the way in which he positions women as sometimes the
same as men, as individuals with natural rights, and sometimes different, and as such subject to men – permit him to secure the apparent
self-presence of the key philosophical concepts of origin, humanity

and power. 'Women' is used in the *Two Treatises* as sometimes different from, sometimes the same as, men, in order to create in the text a movement from a self-present origin in which there is a single humanity of free and equal individuals to a political society based on the distinction between different types of power, in two self-present spheres – the public and private. I intend to show that the inconsistencies of Locke's treatment of 'women', far from being irrelevant as Carole Pateman argues, are vital to the constitution of the liberal division between public and private as it is constructed in the *Two Treatises*. In order to investigate this we shall go through Locke's text closely, looking at how 'women' operates and how it simultaneously makes possible and impossible the self-presence of specific liberal concepts.

Locke's *First Treatise* is mostly concerned with the refutation of Sir Robert Filmer's *Patriarcha* – a defence of the absolute right of the sovereign over his people. The position of women, or more particularly of Eve, is crucial to Locke's refutation of Filmer. Filmer argued that the absolute right of kings was guaranteed by God at the Creation (Filmer, 1991). There is no need for us here to go through the details of Filmer's extraordinary arguments from Scripture concerning the origin of the right of kings to absolute rule. His work is relevant to us here only insofar as it appears in Locke's. According to Locke, '*By the appointment of God*, says Sir Robert, *as soon as Adam* was Created he was Monarch of the World' (Locke, 1960 p. 186, author's emphasis in all quotes except where noted). It will be Locke's task – one he goes to great lengths to accomplish – to show that Filmer's interpretation of Genesis cannot be accepted, principally because Filmer has misunderstood, or overlooked, the part played by Eve at the beginning of the world. To anticipate the conclusion of our discussion of this part of the text, Locke will argue that Filmer supposes that Adam was alone at the origin and that it is this supposition that enables him to posit a single, unified source of power that extends through time, from the beginning of Creation, and across space, across the whole of society without limits. In order to split this power at the origin and to show its limits, Locke will use the position of Eve as *like* Adam, as the same as him, and as therefore participating equally in whatever power Adam may have been granted by God. There was not one at the origin, there were two, according to Locke. And this doubling of identity at the origin will be used by Locke to try to secure his own dream of self-present origin, that of mankind in the state of nature.

We turn, then, to Locke's argument against Filmer's version of Genesis. Locke argues that Filmer elaborates two confused and contradictory ways in which Adam was made 'a King from his Creation'. First, God appointed him monarch of the world as soon as he was created and gave him 'Private Dominion' over all the creatures of the earth, including his children. And second, God appointed Adam monarch of the world because as the father of his children he had the natural right to rule over them (Locke, 1960, pp. 186–190). In both cases the position of Eve will prove decisive against Filmer. And in both cases the form of the refutation is the same: Eve was there; Adam was not alone.

In the first case, Locke argues that the Scripture explicitly states that God gave dominion over the Earth to *them*, not to Adam alone:

> And God blessed them, and God said unto them, be Fruitful and Multiply and Replenish the Earth and subdue it, and have Dominion over the Fish of the Sea, and over the Fowl of the Air, and over every living thing that moveth upon the Earth.
>
> (Locke, 1960, p. 191)

This '*them*', he says, clearly indicates that God's grant of dominion was not made to Adam alone, and that therefore it cannot secure for him the absolute sovereignty over all that Filmer requires of it. Here Eve is used as a double of Adam to split his power at the origin:

> But the Grant being to them ie spoke to *Eve* also, as many interpreters think with reason, that these words were not spoken till *Adam* had his Wife, must she not thereby be Lady, as well as he Lord of the World?
>
> (p. 196)

Eve is simply different from Adam as his double here; she is different only insofar as there are two, not one. She is not different from Adam as his subject; at least, though she may be subject to him this does not alter her status as 'Lady of the World': she is 'not so subjected to him as to hinder her *Dominion* over the Creatures, or *Property* in them' (p. 196). How could she be when the aim is to introduce equality at the origin in order to disperse Adam's power among men, to show that God gave '*them*' dominion and not '*him*'? That this is indeed Locke's object is clear:

> Whatever God gave by the words of this grant [quoted above] it was not to Adam in particular, exclusive of all other Men: whatever *Dominion* he had thereby, it was not a *Private Dominion*, but a Dominion in common with the rest of Mankind.
>
> (p. 196)

Eve is here used to introduce a difference from Adam in the origin that is actually sameness; as the double of Adam she splits the origin and enables the dispersal of Adam's unique power among all 'mankind', among all the other identical individuals at the origin.[2]

However, Locke cannot pass so lightly over Eve's subjection to Adam at the Creation because of the way Filmer builds on the scriptural evidence of his rule over her to make his case for Adam's absolute sovereignty. According to Locke's reading of Filmer, the scriptural case for Adam's power over Eve is made out in the curse that God put on her when she was cast out from the Garden of Eden. As Locke puts it:

The next piece of Scripture we find our A. Builds his Monarchy of *Adam* on, is 3. Gen. 16. *And thy desire shall be to thy Husband, and he shall rule* over *thee. Here we have* (says he) *the Original Grant of Government*, from whence he concludes ... *That the Supream Power is settled in the Fatherhood, and limited to one kind of Government, that is to Monarchy.*

(Locke, 1960, p. 207)

In this case it is hardly possible for Locke to argue against Eve's difference from Adam; it is not possible for him to sustain his thesis that Adam and Eve are the same. However, he does try to minimise the difference between them, as it is clearly important for him to do if he is not to concede Filmer's point, that God granted Adam absolute power in the beginning.

First, Locke argues that these words are a curse from God on Eve, but that since Adam had also disobeyed Him, God was not here dispensing prerogatives and privileges. Adam too 'had his share in the fall' and if, because she was 'a helper in the Temptation, as well as a partner in the Transgression', he was given some superiority over Eve this is a very small thing in comparison with what both were made to suffer. In fact Locke describes Adam's superiority over Eve as 'accidental' (p. 208). In essence, he argues, both are the same, both Adam and Eve sinned, both were expelled from the Garden of Eden. There is nothing in the difference between the man and the woman that gives him the right to power over her; the fact that he *does* have power over her is contingent, accidental, not essential.

Second, he makes the rather obscure argument that actually God is not here making a prescription, He is not telling Eve that she must subordinate herself to Adam; rather He is predicting what *will be* women's lot. And indeed, he argues, women need not subject themselves to their husbands if their marriage contracts permit them to avoid doing so, though it is customary that they will. Furthermore, he concedes, 'there is, I grant, a Foundation in Nature for it', although this is in direct contradiction of all that he has just argued (pp. 209–10). Again, men's power over women is minimised; it is seen as more or less accidental. The way is left open for positioning women much more explicitly as subject to men – there is a foundation in nature for it – when it becomes necessary later in the text, but in the context of Locke's argument against Filmer women's difference from men as their subordinates is minimised where it can't be eliminated.

Finally, we come to the second case Filmer makes for Adam's sovereignty as a grant from God at Creation – that which derives from his natural rights as a father. This is, in Locke's opinion, 'the main basis of all his frame' (p. 212). In response to Filmer, Locke again uses woman as a double of man, this time to split paternal power. According to Locke, the weight of Filmer's case rests on a passage in the Decalogue in which 'the Law that injoyns obedience to Kings is delivered in the Terms, Honour the Father' (p. 220). But, Locke argues:

> had our A. set down this Command without Garbling, as God gave it, and joyned *Mother* to Father, every Reader would have seen that it had made directly against him, and that it was so far from Establishing the *Monarchical Power of the Father*, that it set up the *Mother* equal with him, and injoyn'd nothing but what was due in common, to both Father and Mother . . .
>
> (p. 222)

The power of the father cannot be that of a monarch, Locke concludes, for if the power of the mother is guaranteed by God in an identical way to that of the father,

> he has a Power very far from Monarchical, very far from that Absoluteness our A contends for, when another has over his Subjects the same Power he hath, and by the same Title.
>
> (p. 223)

Again, then, woman – in this case, the mother – is introduced as a double of man – the father. She is the same as him and she serves to divide his power, to deny the possibility that there can have been at the origin, and so forever will be, a sole source of power over all. As such she opens the way for another origin of power – that of mankind in the state of nature.

In order to summarise and conclude this exposition of Locke's refutation of Filmer's account of the origins of political power I will quote Locke's own summary and conclusion of this part of the *First Treatise*. In the quote I have marked (in square brackets) the use Locke makes of the undecidability of woman to move from Filmer's origin as that of a single, unified monarchical power to the origin he prefers, that of a power which is identical in all human individuals, and which is, therefore, single and unified in mankind. 'Woman' as a hymen which allows for both sameness and difference permits the play of identity and difference which produces this shift from self-present origin to self-present origin, while enabling those origins to present themselves as such. As a hymen 'woman' is between two presences; effacing the effect it has on each, it produces both. In Locke's words:

> At last we have got through all that in our A. looks like an Argument for that *Absolute Unlimited Sovereignty* described, Sect. 8. which he supposes in *Adam*, so that Mankind ever since have been all born *Slaves*, without any Title to Freedom. But if *Creation* which gave nothing but a Being, made not *Adam Prince of his Posterity: If Adam, Gen.* 1.28. was not constituted Lord of Mankind, nor had a *Private Dominion* given him exclusive of his Children, but only a Right and Power over the Earth, and Inferiour Creatures in common with the Children of Men [if Eve is the double of Adam, as the same]: If also *Gen* 3.16. God gave not any Political Power to *Adam* over his Wife and Children, but only subjected Eve to *Adam*, as a punishment, or foretold the Subjection of the weaker Sex, in the ordering [of] the common concernments of their Families . . . [if woman is almost the same as man, but perhaps a little different]: And if the Command, *Honour thy Father and Mother*, give it not, but only enjoyns a Duty owing to parents equally . . . [if mothers are the same as fathers]; If all this be so, as I think by what has been said, is very evident, then Man has a *Natural Freedom*, notwithstanding all our A. confidently says to the contrary, since all that share in the same common Nature, Faculties and Powers, are in Nature equal and ought to partake in the same common Rights and Priviledges . . .
> (pp. 226–7)

The importance of the unity of mankind in the state of nature cannot be overestimated in Locke's philosophy. It is this unity, the way in which power is dispersed among individuals who are essentially replicas of each other, which enables him to describe political society as one in which free and equal individuals consent to be ruled. They are able to agree to laws which will be satisfactory to all, which will uphold one public good, because they are in essence identical; as individuals they are fragments of the unity that is mankind. Any differences which individuals may have one from the other, including differences of interpretation and those differences in wealth that Locke introduces in his discussion of property, are irrelevant in the public sphere of political society where only essential characteristics of mankind count. Universal laws are agreed on by representatives of the community who exercise their judgement for the public good:

> thus all private judgement of every particular Member being excluded, the Community comes to be Umpire, by settled standing Rules, indifferent, and the same to all Parties; and by Men having Authority from the Community, for the execution of those Rules . . .
>
> (p. 367)

There is no need actually for each member of the community to participate in the law-making; it is enough that all consent to the laws that are made by the representatives. In fact, Locke assumes that so long as there is no actual rebellion against the government of the day, laws have been tacitly consented to (p. 392). There is no need on Locke's theory for the democratic participation of all in the process of decision-making because so long as the law is truly universal, so long as it holds for all equally, it is just; since all share in the essential qualities of mankind all will recognise their interests in the one public good decided on their behalf.

Differences between individuals are excluded from consideration in the public sphere of political society and become matters of concern only to the individuals themselves in the private sphere on Locke's scheme. And it is here too that the difference which he makes between men and women becomes significant. Woman's difference from and natural subjection to man comes into play as a way of separating the public from the private and of guaranteeing the self-identity of each. Since, however, as we have seen, Locke also makes use of a contradictory meaning of woman as the same as man the separation of public and private is never finally possible.

Women's subjection to men is discussed in the *Second Treatise*, in the context of Locke's analysis of power in the domestic sphere as opposed to political power in the public sphere. Locke needs to show that they are two different things in order to counteract Filmer's theory of power as homogeneous, unified across the social field. He begins by reiterating the point we have seen him use against Filmer's views on creation: 'The *first society* was between Man and Wife', either of whom, according to Locke, could be the 'Master or Mistress' of the household over which they ruled. Locke is so far from asserting the natural subjection of women at this point in the text that he states that '*Conjugal Society* is made by a voluntary Compact between Man and Woman . . .' (p. 362) Here, then, in 'the first society', intermediate between the state of nature and political society, men and women are both apparently free and equal as individuals. However, in political society itself things are rather different:

> But the Husband and Wife, though they have but one common Concern yet having different understandings, will unavoidably sometimes have different wills too; it therefore being necessary, that the last Determination *i.e.* the Rule, should be placed somewhere, it naturally falls to the Man's share, as the abler and stronger.
>
> (Locke, 1960, p. 364)

Here the woman is different from the man and naturally subject to him. Why is this important to Locke? Why must there be one sole authority in the home? In this respect the private sphere is like the public sphere; Locke can conceive of power only as unified, ultimately self-identical.[3] Just as there can be no fundamental differences in the public sphere – consent to the universal law is guaranteed by expelling differences that might result in irreconcilable division – there can be no room for fundamental disagreements in the private sphere. In the case of the former unity is guaranteed, as we have seen, by the self-identity of mankind, including women; in the latter case the self-identity of authority is guaranteed by women's natural difference from men which subjects wives to husbands.

One of the principal objects of Locke's argument against Filmer is that men in the private sphere have sole authority over those aspects of their lives which are their's by natural right. These are included under the title of property, though property for Locke includes more than just wealth; it also includes life, health and liberty (p. 311). These are outside the scope of the law except insofar as the law must be made to protect the rights of citizens in the private sphere (pp. 402–3). Law in the public sphere must presuppose the interests of these private citizens to be essentially identical – since, as we have seen, this is the precondition of consent to universal principles. So it follows

that there should be no fundamental disagreements between citizens in
the private sphere, no irreconcilable differences. If the possibility of
irreconcilable differences in the private sphere were acknowledged, it
would be difficult to sustain the view of the community as essentially
unified and difficult to exclude those differences from consideration in
the public sphere. The self-presence of the one public good would risk
contamination by difference. Clearly, then, there must be no irreconcilable differences in any particular household between 'Master and
Mistress', and there need not be because women, although free and
equal individuals like every other member of the human race are also,
at the same time, subject to men.[4]

Thus, having been positioned as the double of man at the origin in
order to guarantee the essential identity of mankind in the public sphere,
woman is now positioned as different from man in order to guarantee
the essential self-identity of the natural authority exercised by heads
of households in the private sphere. Public and private are rigorously
separated as self-present categories operating according to different
principles and governed by different types of power.

But not quite. Since, as we have seen, this opposition between public and private has been made possible by the undecidability of 'woman',
it is an opposition which can never finally be achieved; its condition
of possibility is also its condition of impossibility. This becomes evident when Locke follows his statement concerning husbands' natural
authority with the following:

> But this reaching but to the things of their common Interest and
> Property, leaves the Wife in the full and free possession of what by
> Contract is her peculiar Right, and gives the Husband no more power
> over her Life, than she has over his. The *Power of the Husband being*
> so far from that of an absolute Monarch, that the *Wife* has, in many
> cases, a Liberty to *separate* from him; where natural Right, or their
> Contract allows it . . .
>
> (Locke, 1960, p. 364)

And he goes on to describe everything else that may be included in
the terms of a marital contract, along with the right to separation:

> Community of Goods, and the Power over them, mutual Assistance,
> and Maintenance, and other things belonging to *Conjugal Society*,
> might be varied and regulated by that Contract, which unites Man
> and Wife in that Society, as far as may consist with Procreation and

the bringing up of Children till they could shift for themselves; nothing being necessary to any Society, that is not necessary to the ends for which it is made.

(p. 365)

Here, then, because woman is both the same as *and* different from man, the marital relation is considered to be *almost all* contractual; the husband's natural authority over the wife which is necessary to the self-identity of the private sphere is minimised. A marriage contract is 'obtained under Politick Government'; it is regulated by law in the public sphere and the Civil Magistrate decides on controversies that might arise between husbands and wives concerning it. In other words, marriage, since it is almost all contractual, is almost all public too. The undecidability of women which makes the separation of public and private possible also means that the public sphere of contract and law is brought into the private domestic sphere of natural care and subordination. Ultimately, it becomes impossible to decide what is public and what is private in the domestic sphere because almost every aspect of the relation between husband and wife may be regulated by contract.[5]

We have seen, then, how 'woman' functions in Locke's text as a Derridean hymen which both makes possible the separation and self-presence of public and private and at the same time makes impossible a rigorous delineation of the two sides of the opposition. If this deconstructive reading of Locke is convincing, then Pateman's understanding of the public and private spheres as based on the fundamental opposition of male and female and as simply opposed to each other in early liberalism is clearly only partially correct; public and private were both opposed and implicated in each other as a result of the undecidability of woman *between* the figure of rational man, free and equal and able to consent to universal principles in the public sphere, and the figure of subordinate woman, concerned only with domestic interests and excluded from the political process. The question remains, however, of the relevance of this reading to feminist theory. At the level of the text I think I have shown that a Derridean approach is useful in opening up possibilities that were not previously noticed, or that were repressed in Pateman's reading of Locke, but there remains the question of the theoretical, and indeed, the historical relevance of this reading. It is to a consideration of these questions that we shall now turn.

FEMINISM AND THE UNDECIDABILITY OF 'WOMEN' IN THE *TWO TREATISES*

In this section I want to argue that the deconstructive reading of Locke's text I am proposing here is useful to a feminist account of liberalism because it enables us to think about the *instability* of its central categories and oppositions, in particular of the oppressive binary opposition between public and private. This instability has always been a feature of liberalism, from its beginnings in the seventeenth century. In order to see the advantages of this for feminism we need to break with the idea of political theory as reflective of socio-economic relations and look on it as an attempt to hegemonise social meanings, to articulate them according to specific political projects. Political theory does not reflect already given social relations; it is part of attempts to institute them. In the case of feminism, such attempts have involved opening up the liberal undecidability of women.

Liberalism, Feminism and Anti-patriarchalism

Before we address the question of the feminist use of this undecidability, however, we must first consider the relationship between feminism and liberalism more generally, and in particular their relationship in early modernity. A feminist understanding of this relationship sometimes expressed before the critique of liberalism as masculinist became so prominent was that liberalism was a condition of possibility of feminism: once it is established that all humans should be treated equally, women's political and legal subordination to men then becomes contradictory, both within liberalism itself and in the social and political institutions of modern society in which it is the dominant ideology (Mitchell, in Phillips, 1987a, p. 31; Eisenstein, 1988, p. 4). There are, however, two simple problems with this argument.

In the first place, a good deal hangs on what is taken to count as feminism.[6] Women writers began to work out what Denise Riley refers to as 'a formal alignment of sex against sex' as early as the fourteenth century in a genre which defended women against misogyny and recommended their retreat from society in order to pursue the religious devotions that would ensure their suffering at men's hands would be rewarded in the afterlife (Riley, 1988, pp. 10–11). These themes re-emerge in the late seventeenth century when women writers, often publishing anonymously, began to take up the theme of male domination in unprecedented numbers. We may agree, then, that the beginning of feminism as a significant social movement was coincidental with the beginning of liberalism, provided that we see these writers as feminists. They cannot be unequivocally categorised as such since, as we shall see, they very often accepted men's rights as head of households and they did not contest men's pre-eminence in the public sphere. On the other hand, however, they did defend women against slander and they demanded 'rational' education, generally in order to fulfil their tasks as wives and mothers, but sometimes, as in the case of Aphra Behn and Damaris Cudwoth, for the sake of their 'masculine', artistic and intellectual talents (Goreau, 1985). It seems reasonable, then, to identify such women as feminists on the grounds that they advocated women's just demands and, at the very least, explicitly countered misogyny (Ferguson, 1985, p. xi).

Given that a feminist movement did emerge in seventeeth-century England, then, the second problem arises: since all these writers were writing around the same time as Locke, they could not be said to be inspired by, or dependent on, liberalism as a condition of possibility of their endeavours in any straightforward way since liberal principles themselves were highly contested at this time and far from established as a necessary framework within which to consider political rights. And in fact many early feminists were Royalists, openly hostile to Locke's philosophy. This is true, for example, of the most prominent and systematic of these writers, Mary Astell, who was a High Church Tory and who therefore situated herself directly in opposition to the terms of Lockean liberalism. As we shall see, Astell is a complicated writer who addressed her readers in an extremely ironical style so that she actually has a much more complicated relationship to liberalism than her overt political position would suggest; nevertheless, it is clear that she does not argue for women's equality on the basis of its universal, humanist principles as has sometimes been suggested (Mitchell, 1987, p. 31).

However, if liberalism was not a condition of possibility of feminism in any direct way, the coincidental emergence of a significant movement of women against male domination and of liberalism as a political philosophy with direct social and political import suggests that they may be linked in another way: as responses to the social and political upheavals of that particular time and place, to the English Revolution.

Following Claude Lefort, Ernesto Laclau and Chantal Mouffe suggest that feminism, like other modern social movements, was made possible by the extension of the principle of equality instituted by the

French Revolution. This principle enabled the redescription of relations of subordination as relations of oppression on the basis of 'the
rights inherent to every human being' (Laclau and Mouffe, 1985,
p. 154). For Laclau and Mouffe, then, Mary Wollstonecraft is the first
feminist because she explicitly argued for the equality of the sexes on
the basis of human rights. In the light of our considerations concerning feminism before the French Revolution, this designation of
Wollstonecraft as the first seems unjustified, though it is not uncom-
mon (see, for example, M. Brody's introduction to the Penguin edition
of *Vindication of the Rights of Woman*, p. 1 [Wollstonecraft, 1992]).
Certainly, as a radical, Wollstonecraft is clearly opposed to anything
less than complete equality between the sexes, although unlike contemporary feminists she thinks the sexes should operate largely in different
spheres; in comparison, earlier women writers do seem somewhat confused about the legitimate extent of men's power over women. However, it is clear that if we take feminism to be a movement against the
male domination of women, we cannot deny these writers this status
and there was a feminist movement before the French Revolution.
Nevertheless, I want to suggest here that Lefort's theory can be used
to understand the conditions of possibility of feminism, and also of
liberalism, providing that we understand the English situation in the
seventeenth century as exhibiting some of the features he describes in
terms of the democratic revolution.

It would seem that for Lefort there are two distinct moments in the
democratic revolution. The first moment he specifically dates to the
French Revolution, but arguably it could be applied to modernity more
generally and therefore to the English Revolution too: it is the moment when the King lost his head. According to Lefort, in the absolute monarchies of the beginning of modernity, power – the power of
the state which was removed from and set against civil society – knowledge and the law were united in the body of the King. Both mortal
and immortal, as Lefort puts it, 'His power pointed towards an uncon-
ditional, other-worldly pole, while at the same time he was, in his
own person, the guarantor and representative of the unity of the king-
dom' (Lefort, 1988, pp. 16–17). When the King lost his head, society
lost this unity and power became 'an empty place' which no individual or group can completely fill. Once the transcendental guarantee
has been destroyed, power, knowledge and the law are 'disincorporated',
they are separated and the relationship between them becomes an arena
of conflict (Lefort, 1986, p. 255). No longer unconditionally guaranteed, power is continually challenged by right – by knowledge and

law; the essence of law can no longer be ascertained with certainty and its legitimacy is subject to constant debate; and knowledge itself is always open to question, in its conclusions and in its very foundations (Lefort, 1988, pp. 17–18). In Lefort's words, 'democracy is instituted and sustained by the *dissolution of the markers of certainty*' (p. 19; author's emphasis).

What unites Lefort's account of the democratic revolution with the history of the emergence of feminism and liberalism in early modern England is anti-patriarchalism. As we have seen in Locke's attack on Filmer and in his substantive political philosophy, seventeenth-century liberalism involved a thorough questioning of the legitimacy and limits of sovereignty and the argument that what had previously been taken to be divinely guaranteed authority should be replaced by contractually established political power. Related to this questioning of divine sovereignty there was a much less voluble and less effective feminist questioning of the patriarchal power in the family to which it had been metaphorically linked. Although divinely sanctioned rule was not as entrenched in England as in France, it was nevertheless challenged and finally overthrown in 1688 and the contestation of power that accompanied the transformation in government of the Glorious Revolution may well been characterised in Lefort's terms as democratic.

The term 'patriarchy' is often used rather loosely by contemporary feminists to refer to the power of men over women, but it also has a very precise use, meaning the power of the father; that is, the power of a male figure who is the head of a group whose members are related, either by blood or marriage, including both women and other men. Pre-modern society is sometimes called patriarchal because, although the power of fathers as heads of households was not absolute, medieval society was organised into kinship groups headed by hereditary lords who had virtually complete economic and political power over those over whom they ruled, including the right of life or death (Weber, 1982, p. 296; Nicholson, 1986, p. 143). It is not strictly accurate to name them such since noble households also ruled over, and depended on the work of, those who were not members of the family; it is, in fact, only metaphorically that the term 'patriarchal' can be used to describe this type of social organisation. And it is only in a metaphorical sense that a sovereign can be thought of as patriarchal since medieval society was composed of many such kinship groups; obviously a monarch cannot literally be related to all his subjects. Nevertheless, it was in opposition to a theory legitimating sovereignty as patriarchy that Locke developed his liberalism, and the questioning of sovereignty as patriarchy to which he contributed also, by extension, problematised the patriarchy of the household.

According to Gordon Schochet, patriarchalism – a formal theory legitimating patriarchy – was not actually explicitly elaborated until the early seventeenth century with the institution of the absolutism of James I (Schochet, 1975, p. 86). The view that political power was in some way derived from natural origins in the family had been taken for granted since at least the sixteenth century and, as we will see, patriarchy was implicit in many practices throughout the Middle Ages, but it was only made explicit when James I took the throne and it reached its fullest expression when Sir Robert Filmer's apology for divinely sanctioned monarchy was published as part of an attempt to restore the monarchy (pp. 37–8). It only really became prominent, then, when it was challenged by contractual theories of political obligation and political revolution. Although absolute monarchy was brief in England in comparison with absolute monarchy in France (Ruggiero, 1959, pp. 4–11), the fact that patriarchalism was only fully set out in England once the legitimacy of the sovereign came to be questioned, once power was no longer taken to be embodied in the person of the King, confirms Lefort's thesis that in modernity political power is always contestable: Filmer's patriarchalism was necessarily self-defeating – the fact that *Patriarcha* needed to be written as a defence of the divine right of the sovereign meant that it could not be accepted – and overstrained. There had been analogies between fathers as the heads of households and kings as the heads of state throughout the Middle Ages, but what Filmer argued was not that the sovereign was *like* a father, but that kings should actually be taken to *be* the fathers of their people. Although this now seems ridiculous (and indeed it seems that not even Filmer thought Charles I was directly descended from Adam, though others did argue this [Schochet, 1975, pp. 153–8]), it should be noted that his contemporaries, including Locke of course, took the theory seriously enough to marshal extensive and detailed arguments against it. As several commentators have noted, Filmer's arguments are laughable not because they are philosophically wrong – they could still be taken seriously if this were the case – but because the collapse of patriarchalism was so complete that liberalism set the framework of modern political culture and we no longer think in Filmer's terms; we struggle to see his problems and solutions as worth consideration. Locke's separation of political and familial power as different in kind, and the institutional separation between the public sphere of the state and the private sphere of civil society that accompanied it historically, have provided the terms within which modern political theorists have tried to think their social and political situation (Schochet, 1975, pp. 268–76; Nicholson, 1986, pp. 131–5).

What this means is that liberalism has become hegemonic. As Laclau and Mouffe have pointed out, Lefort's theory of democracy as contestation has an intimate relationship with hegemony. According to Lefort, we must distinguish between two senses of the political in modernity. The first, *la politique*, refers to the politics of liberal-democratic theory; it is the politics of representative government which liberalism confines to the public sphere, however it is delineated. The second, *le politique*, refers to politics which institute new social forms. *Le politique* concerns the articulation of symbols, the means by which, according to Lefort, humans establish their relation to the world (Lefort, 1988, p. 222). The concept of *le politique* allows us, then, to go beyond the narrow liberal-democratic view of politics to see the process by which the very terms of that politics, the oppositions between public and private and between women and men with which we are concerned in this study, have been defined, articulated and contested in attempts to institute new social and political practices. As Laclau and Mouffe have pointed out, a theory of politics as *le politique* requires a theory of hegemony because it raises the question of how relatively stable social forms are achieved. Although, as we have seen, on Lefort's account the meaning of social practices can not be finally fixed, there must always be a *partial* fixity if there is to be any meaning at all; even for contestation to take place, social forms must be relatively stable (Laclau and Mouffe, 1985, p. 112). Precisely because there is no assured end to the contestability of the social, hegemonic projects become both possible and necessary (p. 187). The contestation of patriarchalism by liberalism did not, then, mean *an end* to the relationship between power, knowledge and law with the emptying of the place of the sovereign, it meant rather the articulation of a new relationship between them in terms of the liberal distinction between public and private.

This liberal opposition between public and private, conflating as it does the private sphere of civil society and the domestic sphere is, of course, precisely the problem that liberalism has bequeathed to feminism, the problem with which modern feminism is, arguably, centrally concerned. What the public/private distinction represents is the liberal redescription of patriarchy, a redescription which confined patriarchy to the private domestic sphere and established that political power was to be exercised only in the public sphere. In early modernity, however, liberalism and feminism shared the contestation of patriarchalism which ultimately made liberal hegemony possible.

Although patriarchalism was not made explicit in England until the seventeenth century, it was, as I have mentioned, implicit in social and political practices, including the law, religious worship and so on throughout the Middle Ages. For example, women tried for murdering their husbands were tried for treason up to the nineteenth century (Corrigan and Sayer, 1985, pp. 36–7). And, as another example, the catechism introduced in 1549 used the analogy between the respect owed to fathers and the duty to obey social superiors in a very similar way to Filmer's formal political theory:

> My duty to my neighbour is to love him as myself, and to do to all men as I would they should do unto me: to love, honour and succour my father and mother: to submit myself to all my governors, teachers, spiritual pastors and masters; to order myself lowly and reverently to all my betters . . .
>
> (quoted in Laslett, 1971, p. 186)

Patriarchalism, then, was not just an abstract theory used to justify the divine right of kings; it could be used in this way only because it was already concretely grounded in a social order in which the power of male heads of households was practically taken for granted as natural and God-given. Both liberalism and feminism were made possible by the challenge to the taken-for-grantedness of patriarchalism which took place throughout Europe in early modernity.

It is widely agreed by historians of the period that the Protestant Reformation resulted in a general undermining of the previously accepted grounds of social and political authority. First, traditional claims of religious authority, a central support of patriarchalism, as we have seen, were destroyed by the institution of the direct relationship between believer and God practised by Protestants. The single most important theme in this respect, common to both liberalism and feminism, was freedom of conscience. From a liberal perspective, freedom of conscience gives rise to the familiar liberal arguments for toleration, the separation of Church and State and also, less directly, to the idea that an individual must have a natural right to a sphere of freedom outside state interference (Ruggiero, 1959, pp. 13–23). The idea of freedom of conscience had a less direct, but no less important, place in early feminism: if every individual must decide for herself what she believes, it is simply rationally impossible to submit in thought to what one finds unjust. None of the early feminists argued from this premise that women should not therefore have to obey men, but the conclusion that men's power over women might not be legitimate could not be avoided. For Mary Astell, for example:

> ... tho the Order of the World requires an *Outward* Respect and Obedience from some to others, yet the Mind is free, nothing but Reason can oblige it, 'tis out of reach of the most absolute Tyrant.
>
> (Astell, 1986a, p. 110)

For early feminists, the only way to avoid tyranny was to avoid marriage; they did not dispute the right of husbands and fathers to expect women's obedience, but the idea that ultimately women had only their own conscience to answer to was an opening in the unquestioning acceptance of patriarchal power in the household.

The philosophical questioning of all received dogma initiated by Descartes, which also challenged patriarchalism, was a direct extension of the questioning of religious authority; both religious and philosophical questioning relied on the same method of questioning all that could not be apprehended as true by the individual mind (Ruggiero, 1959, p. 21). As Ruggiero argues, freedom of thought was not an empty declamation for early liberals, it was not simply tautological, but rather 'a declaration of war against the tyranny of schools, Churches, States, and customs, over conscience' (p. 23). It was particularly the questioning of custom and tradition initiated by the rationalist methods of Cartesianism which influenced early feminists. As a philosophy which, unlike the scholastic doctrines it displaced, was in principle accessible to any rational thinker, even those, like women, who had not been formally educated, Cartesian rationalism and the principles of the new science were enthusiastically adopted by Aphra Behn, Damaris Cudworth, Margaret Cavendish and all those who demanded a rational education for women (Ferguson, 1985, pp. 12–13). It was particularly attractive to early feminists since it facilitated a questioning which did not directly challenge the political and religious authorities they respected, although the Cartesian refusal to accept any truth based on less than rational principles made it virtually impossible for those inspired by the method to forgo questioning justifications of women's position based on arguments from tradition or custom. For early feminists the sexes were equal in rational abilities and any social differences between men and women which did not allow women to develop their capacity for

reason to the full were almost inevitably brought into question
(Smith, 1982, pp. 10–12). It was rationalism that inspired Mary
Astell's feminist convictions, for example, rather than the radical politics and religious questioning which she forcefully resisted (Perry,
1986, pp. 331–2).

The very fact that such a large number of women began publishing
their writing in the second half of the seventeenth century, though
they often did not sign their work for the sake of 'modesty', indicates
a weakening of patriarchalism as an ideology justifying male power
and privilege. However, patriarchy as the practice of the power of the
father over the household cannot be said to have been weakened at
this time. On the contrary, following the Reformation a new form of
patriarchy sanctioned by Puritanism was institutionalised; male heads
of households, rather than the clergy, were given responsibility for
their families' spiritual well-being and as such they were to be obeyed
(Wiesner, 1993, p. 243). As a justification of male power, patriarchalism
was contested by early feminists, albeit somewhat half-heartedly, but
patriarchy in the domestic sphere survived and took on a new form in
seventeenth-century England.

Unlike the anti-patriarchalism of liberalism, then, feminist anti-
patriarchalism was circumscribed and there was no revolution in the
household to match the revolution in government. Nevertheless, feminism emerged, almost unwillingly it seems in retrospect, in response
to the weakening of patriarchalism. In this respect, then, both feminism and liberalism share their beginnings in the contestation of divinely sanctioned power, a contestation which, at least in this respect,
we can see both as participating in, and helping create the conditions
for, democratic revolution in Lefort's sense of the term as the dissolution of certainty and the institution of continuous contestation.

However, on Lefort's theory there is a second element of the democratic revolution which did not feature in the English Revolution as it
did in the French: the institution of the principle of equal rights. For
Lefort, the democratic revolution instituted a form of the social in which
rights are central to the legitimacy of government. The democratic
revolution is not just the contestation of power, but its contestation in
the name of the rights of man. When power, knowledge and the law
become 'disincorporated' in the first moment of the democratic revolution, the second moment becomes possible: right is freed from its
identification with power and there is nothing which can limit in advance the scope of claims made in the name of human rights. A new
form of the social is introduced in that democratic rights are poten-

tially subversive of established political, social or economic relations in the name of the essential liberty and equality of man (Lefort, 1986, pp. 256–7).

Democracy as a new form of the social organised around legitimate claims to human rights was introduced by the French Revolution; the English Revolution was not democratic in this sense. Of course, Lockean liberalism justified its demands for limiting political power in terms of the natural rights of man, but the Declaration of Rights of 1689 was very different from the Declaration of the Rights of Man of 1789. Civil rights and limited political rights *were* formally instituted in 1689, and they were claimed as the 'ancient rights and liberties' of the subjects of the king which had been contravened by James II, but none of the articles of the constitution were individually claimed as rights, far less as rights intrinsic to human beings as such; for the most part they were statements of the powers of parliament and the judiciary, which were to remain independent of the monarchy (Ashby, 1968, pp. 277–80). This is in sharp contrast to the Declaration of 1789, boldly beginning as it does with Article I: 'Men are born and live free and equal as regards their rights. Social distinctions can be based only on the common interest' (Ruggiero, 1959, p. 66). With this assertion, as Lefort sees it, the Declaration of the Rights of Man constituted man for the first time as a political subject whose essence it is to declare his rights (Lefort, 1986, pp. 256–7). It formally instituted 'the right to have rights', in Arendt's phrase, and so began 'an adventure whose outcome is unpredictable' since rights can always be used to challenge social subordination however it is instituted (Lefort, 1988, p. 37).

The English Revolution was democratic in terms of the first aspect of Lefort's theory of democratic revolution, then, in that it emptied the place of power of the absolute monarch, so beginning the irresolvable contestation of modern power, but not in the second sense in that it did not institute the possibility of contesting that power in the name of human rights. And just as seventeenth-century liberalism and seventeenth-century feminism share the first aspect, so both share the absence of the second aspect of the democratic revolution. As we have seen, the liberal revolution was not democratic in this sense, and nor was seventeenth-century feminism: early feminists did not couch their arguments in terms of rights and for the most part they were distinctly hostile to such arguments. Mary Wollstonecraft was certainly the first *democratic* feminist, and feminism as a democratic movement did not begin in England until demands were made for political, legal and eventually social rights for women in the nineteenth century.

From the use of Lefort's theory of democracy, it is clear, then, that seventeenth-century liberalism and early feminism were not directly related insofar as the first was the condition of the second, but they were indirectly related insofar as the contestation of patriarchalism was the condition of possibility of both. There is, however, a more direct relationship between the two with which we will be concerned in the rest of this book. We have seen how much less successful feminism was at establishing itself as a relatively stable hegemonic formation than liberalism and, as a result of this uneven development, feminism has always found it necessary to challenge liberalism on its own terms, to rework the categories and principles of the hegemonic discourse in order to articulate and institute its own counter-hegemonic project. In particular, feminism has used the liberal undecidability of women as it has been put into play in modern social and political institutions in order to create better conditions for women. Liberalism is not the condition of possibility of feminism, but historically it has provided many of the tools feminists have used.

In early modernity, however, while liberalism was undoubtedly a hegemonic project, and a highly successful one, feminism cannot really be seen as a project or movement which was counter-hegemonic to liberalism; women writing on sexual inequality made very few proposals for concrete change and little attempt to institute the proposals they did make (perhaps unsurprisingly since it was considered so immodest even for women to write, far less on the topic of women's subordination). Furthermore, for these women, early feminism had only the slightest relationship with liberalism. Although many future feminists would be no more in favour of liberalism than their predecessors in the seventeenth century, though for very different reasons, in actually trying to institute concrete changes feminists in the nineteenth and twentieth centuries would find it impossible to ignore liberalism since it had been formative of the very institutions they sought to change. In the seventeenth century, however, the only feminist writer really to engage with liberalism was Mary Astell, undoubtedly the most systematic and philosophical feminist thinker of the time, and she did so only in a relatively peripheral way, which drew attention to Locke's use of the undecidability of women without engaging further with the emerging hegemonic discourse.

Locke's Ethico-political Decision and Feminist Deconstruction of the *Two Treatises*

To return, then, to the relationship between Locke's *Two Treatises* and the beginnings of feminism, it is clear that Locke's text should be understood as part of the hegemonic project of early liberalism. Following Laslett, it seems to be beyond reasonable doubt that the *Two Treatises* was written to instigate revolution against absolutist monarchy even though it was only published later, as a response to Filmer, in order to legitimise the Revolution of 1688 (Locke, 1960, ch. 3). Locke wrote, then, not as an academic philosopher but as a political activist and he was concerned not just with philosophical justifications for the limitation of patriarchal power to the domestic sphere, but also with ensuring that a strict separation between public and private was actually instituted in practice.

As part of this hegemonic project, as we have seen in the deconstruction of the *Two Treatises*, Locke used the undecidability of women to establish the opposition between public and private. However, having used the term 'women' as an undecidable, he did not want the status of women to be ambiguous and he attempted to close off this undecidability. In Derridean terms, Locke made an ethical-political decision to think women as presence (Derrida, 1988, p. 116). Ultimately, he tried to fix the category of women as a single, self-present identity, as naturally subject to man. That this is so is clear from the way in which, having discussed women's position as subordinate in the domestic sphere, he never once mentions them again, either as different or essentially the same as men, throughout the long discussion of political society. The clear and distinct opposition between public and private at which Locke aims cannot be achieved, since it is dependent on the undecidability of women between the two, but Locke assumes that it is possible, that it has been achieved in his philosophy and that the individuals who are to count in the considerations of the public good are (male) heads of households.

In this respect, then, I am in agreement with Carole Pateman's reading of the *Two Treatises*: to the extent that Locke decided to position women as naturally subordinate in the domestic sphere, excluding them from participation in the public sphere, Pateman's reading of the text is apposite. Where I am in disagreement with Pateman is that, like the other feminist critics of liberalism as masculinist who reproduce its binary oppositions, she makes the same ethico-theoretical decision as classical liberalism itself. She represses possibilities that may be drawn

out of the undecidability of women in the *Two Treatises* in favour of
the decision which Locke himself makes. She duplicates Locke's own
attempt at the closure of his text in favour of women's subordination.
Clearly she does so as part of a very different hegemonic project from
that in which Locke himself was engaged; her decision is made as part
of a feminist critique of liberal political theory and is intended as a
first step towards replacing it with a more comprehensive theory, one
which will recognise that the positioning of women as subordinate in
the private sphere is *political*, not natural. But to the extent that she
reproduces the binary oppositions which Locke attempted to close, *as if
they were actually closed*, as if Locke had succeeded in the task he set
himself, it seems that her perspective remains so much within the categories of liberalism itself that nothing new can ever be generated there.

Mary Astell approached Locke's liberalism in a rather different way
from Pateman, in the way in which I will argue in the rest of this
book that feminism as counter-hegemonic to liberalism has generally
approached it: she made use of the undecidability of the term 'women'
in liberalism, though not necessarily self-consciously. Of course,
'undecidability' is a technical term of Derridean philosophy; what Astell
does strictly speaking is to show the contradictions and inconsistencies in Locke's thought concerning women rather than its undecidability,
the productive oscillation of the term 'women' between two meanings.
Nevertheless, for reasons of her own, Astell is not concerned actually
to analyse Locke's philosophy in detail as contradictory and therefore
as invalid; what she does is to point to the inconsistencies in his work,
as a way of dismissing liberalism certainly, but also as a rhetorical
strategy which makes use of those inconsistencies to make a point
which she herself, from her own premises, could not make: that women
and men should be equal, even within the institution of marriage. It is
in this respect, then, that Astell uses the liberal undecidability of women
productively, as will future feminists, rather than simply pointing up
the inconsistency of liberalism's view of women as a way of dismissing it altogether.

There is an extreme tension in the writings of Mary Astell, between
her feminism and her political and religious convictions. Her religious
convictions are such that she finds herself bound to accept marriage as
a sacred institution in which it has been ordained by God that women
should obey their husbands. All unhappily married women can hope
for is that by doing their duty they might be able to civilise 'one who
proves perhaps so much worse than a Brute' or at least to advance
towards 'perfection' (Astell, 1986a, pp. 130–1). On the other hand,

the whole tone of *Some Reflections upon Marriage* is such to suggest that she does not find men's use of their authority acceptable or justified, concerned as she is to draw the reader's attention to men's abuses of their power and their lack of respect for women. And it is her disapproval of such marriage that leads her to make her only concrete proposal for reform: to set up the secular equivalent of a convent to which women could retire instead of marrying, in order to cultivate themselves and to do good works in the world (Astell, 1986b). The tension in Astell's thought is again evident in the relation between her political position and her feminist beliefs, since as a Tory she was at least as much concerned to defend unquestioning allegiance to the sovereign as she was unwilling to accord the same privileges to a husband. She argued, for example, that:

> She who Elects a Monarch for Life, who gives him an Authority she cannot recall however he misapply it, who puts her Fortune and Person entirely in his Powers ... had need be very sure that she does not make a Fool her Head, nor a Vicious Man her Guide and Pattern ...
>
> (Astell, 1986a, p. 104)

A woman must be very careful whom she marries because rebellion against authority is unacceptable; authority cannot be based on mere force, according to Astell, but nor can it be justly overthrown:

> I love Justice too much to wish Success and continuance to usurpations, which tho' submitted to out of Prudence, and for Quietness sake, yet leave every Body free to regain their lawful Right whenever they have Power and Opportunity
>
> (p. 131)

However, although wives must submit to the authority of their husbands, for the sake of 'order':

> A meer obedience, such is paid only to Authority, and not out of Love and a sense of the Justice and Reasonableness of the Command, will be of uncertain Tenure.
>
> (p. 104)

What look from a contemporary point of view like confusions in Astell's thinking stem from the fact that she is trying to do the impossible: to

defend what should not need, and cannot be, defended, that is the un-
questioned legitimacy of the divine right of kings, and at the same
time to question men's natural superiority and right to rule over women
whilst nevertheless accepting the duty of wives to submit to their husbands. Other women writers of the time adopt a similar, though less
explicitly elaborated, line to Astell's, and therefore also exhibit, to a
lesser extent, the tension in Astell's work. All the early feminists clearly
stipulated that they did not seek to take men's place, nor to overturn
the 'Superiority and Inferiority' essential to a good marriage, but that
they simply wanted women to enjoy an increased respect and
independence based on their improved education within the already
existing social structures (Smith, 1982, p. 107). And it is in the light of
these tensions in Astell's and others' thinking that we should understand
the following equivocal and often quoted statement, evidently directed
at Lockean liberalism and what Astell took to be its seditious aims:

> If Absolute Sovereignty be not necessary in a State, how comes it
> to be so in a Family? or if in a Family why not in a State since no
> Reason can be alledg'd for the one that will not hold more strongly
> for the other? If the Authority of the Husband so far as it extends is
> sacred and inalienable, why not of the Prince? ... *If All Men are
> born free*, how is it that all Women are born slaves?
>
> (Astell, 1986a, p. 76)

While Astell is clearly mocking the inconsistencies of Locke's treatment of women here, her own unresolved position on the 'sacred and
inalienable' authority of the husband is such that she cannot quite be
read as defending that authority; although ostensibly she is defending
the divine right of the sovereign, the phrase can just as easily be read
(as, for example, Juliet Mitchell has read it [1987, p. 31]), as arguing
against the analogous authority of the husband, and therefore of the
sovereign too. Astell seems, then, to be attacking liberalism for its
contradictions, but at the same time she is actually *using* the liberal
undecidability of women as both 'men' (human) and women, almost
without recognising it herself it would seem, to show up the injustice
of husbands' arbitrary rule over wives. Astell therefore opens up the
undecidability of women in Locke's text which he himself attempted
to deny, making evident the repressed possibility that women might be
essentially the same as men and that authority in the private sphere
might be political not natural. And in this respect her writings provide
an example of the way in which feminism as a movement has opened

up liberalism to allow for the possibility of reworking its categories and principles to contest women's subordination, of how feminists have problematised the position of women in liberalism, *from within its own terms*, such that its categories and principles may be used in hegemonic projects to institute somewhat different social and political relations from those instituted by liberalism itself.

To conclude this chapter, then, we have seen how useful Carole Pateman's reading of Locke's *Two Treatises* has been for an understanding of women's position in liberal political theory and practice. She has shown how women have been excluded from the supposedly universal liberal principles of liberty and equality by their subordination in the private sphere. Furthermore, she has shown how the meaning of those public principles is dependent on their opposition to the meaning of the private sphere as exemplified by the role of women. She has shown the interdependence of the two spheres and why it is so difficult to think of women as the individuals of liberal political theory. Her reading of Locke's text is nevertheless limited in important ways, notably in the understanding it allows of feminist responses to women's position in modernity. Pateman's view of liberal political theory as reflective of socio-economic change means that she ascribes to it too much fixity; she overlooks the instability of its central categories and oppositions and the opportunities this instability provides for feminism. As we shall see in the following chapters, feminism has worked within the categories and oppositions of the liberal social formation of modernity, challenging them and attempting to remake them in a new social formation that will be less oppressive to women. While for Astell and her contemporaries liberalism was challenging and important but did not impose itself as the hegemonic formation that had to be addressed, for later feminists liberalism was impossible to overlook.

4 The Democratisation of Liberalism

Although there are some continuities – liberalism always validates its conclusions with reference to the universal principles of liberty and equality, it is always concerned with the individual and it always opposes public and private – there are also significant differences between liberalism in the seventeenth and the nineteenth centuries. In this chapter we shall look at John Stuart Mill's work which, I shall argue, broke with Locke's version of liberalism in at least two important ways, whilst nevertheless remaining within the tradition. First, for Mill, the public/private opposition is drawn *within* the private domestic sphere, around the individual. This represents a significant break with Locke because in Mill's version of liberalism the individual is not masculine. For Mill the individual is *actually* disembodied and unsexed, its gender-neutrality is not illusory as feminist critics of liberalism as masculinist would have it. On Mill's theory, the individual can be both masculine and feminine; there is no need to choose between them as there was for Locke. Second, Mill broke with classical liberalism insofar as he articulated his version of liberalism with democracy and so allowed for difference in the public sphere. The public sphere is not the sphere of universal reason for Mill as it was for Locke; it is also a sphere in which different perspectives, including women's, must be represented.

J.S. MILL, *THE SUBJECTION* (AND THE UNDECIDABILITY) *OF WOMEN*

Pateman's reading of Mill's Liberal Feminism

In this section we shall again approach the question of the inherent masculinity of liberal categories through the work of Carole Pateman, as the feminist critic of liberalism as masculinist who is most attuned to the link between political philosophy and social and political institutions. (1) Pateman argues that despite Mill's radicalism, the way in which he extended the (supposedly) universal liberal principles of freedom and equality to women in *The Subjection of Women*, ultimately he failed to challenge the liberal association between women, love and unpaid care in the home and its opposition to men, justice and paid work outside the home.

Although Mill used liberalism to argue that women's subordination to men was unjust and archaic, an arbitrary abuse of power over rational individuals, and that as such women should have the vote and be allowed to follow a profession and interests in the public sphere, ultimately he assumed that, given the choice, women would choose to be wives and mothers and that they should not then work outside the home:

> Like a man when he chooses a profession, so, when a woman marries, it may in general be understood that she makes a choice of the management of a household, and the bringing up of a family, as the first call upon her exertions, during as many years of her life as may be required for the purpose; and that she renounces, not all other objects and occupations, but all which are not consistent with the requirements of this.
>
> (Mill, 1989b, pp. 164–5)

In fact, although Pateman does not mention this, he goes so far as to argue that in such a situation the man's authority in the home will follow *naturally* from his role as breadwinner: 'There will naturally . . . be a more potential voice on the side, whichever it is, that brings the means of support.' (pp. 156–7)

According to Pateman, what this means is that Mill, as an exemplary liberal theorist, upholds the liberal opposition between the public and the private which is also an opposition between masculine and feminine. On the one hand, he applies liberal political principles to women's position in the private sphere and so challenges the opposition between them, implying that the family is conventional, not natural. But on the other hand, he reinstates women firmly in the private domestic sphere with all its traditional feminine associations of love and care for particular others opposed, as it is, to the public sphere of universal principles of justice (Pateman, 1989b, pp. 129–31).

On Pateman's account, women cannot be the individuals of liberal political theory because for Mill, in order to realise his full potential as 'a moral, spiritual and social being' an individual must participate fully in the political and economic since for Mill, as indeed for Locke, the individual gains identity as a fully rational being concerned with the universal good only by opposition to the feminine private world of care for particular others. As we shall see, there is indeed considerable scope for this reading of Mill's liberalism, but I want to argue nevertheless that it is a misreading. Although Mill's text does reproduce the opposition between a feminine domestic sphere and a masculine public sphere, it is not the case that for him the individual is exclusively masculine. In order to arrive at this conclusion Pateman has had to overlook what she initially recognises as the ambiguities and inconsistencies of Mill's text, as she did in her reading of Locke's work. She has to ignore the way in which he tries to extend the principles of liberty and equality previously associated with the public sphere into the private domestic sphere and the way in which he therefore calls into question both women's 'feminine' status as subordinate to men and the meaning of the domestic sphere itself. If we look more closely at these inconsistencies and make a deconstructive reading of Mill's work we find that the oppositions between public and private, men and women, masculinity and feminine, are neither as stable nor mutually exclusive as the feminist critique of liberalism as masculinist supposes.

On Liberty and *The Subjection of Women*

Here we shall look more closely at the inconsistencies of Mill's text concerning the status of women. We can identify at least three ways in which women are described in the text. First, women are described as unknown and unknowable under the present conditions of their subordination to men. In Mill's words,

> I deny that anyone knows, or can know, the nature of the two sexes, as long as they have only been seen in their present relation to one another ... What is now called the nature of women is an artificial thing – the result of forced repression in some directions, unnatural stimulation in others.
>
> (Mill, 1989b, pp. 138–9)

Second, women are described as essentially the same as men. 'Women' are subsumed under the generic category 'human' and it is argued that, like men, their desire for individual freedom overrides virtually every other consideration. According to Mill, 'After the primary necessities of food and raiment, freedom is the first and strongest want of human nature. (Mill, 1989b, p. 212) And,

He who would rightly appreciate the worth of personal independence as an element of happiness, should consider the value he himself puts upon it as an ingredient of his own. . . . Let him rest assured that whatever he feels on this point, women feel in a fully equal degree.

(pp. 212–13)

Third, women are described as different from men in their current character and capacities. Despite Mill's closely argued claim that men cannot know women so long as women are subordinate to them because in such a situation women are unlikely to reveal their true characters (pp. 140–3), he nevertheless makes extensive generalisations concerning women's interests (pp. 132–3), their concern for the feelings of individuals over the general good (p. 204), their intuitive grasp of details (pp. 173–5), and so on. For Mill there is a feminine character which is clearly distinguishable from the masculine.

There are clear inconsistencies, then, in the way in which Mill uses the term 'women' as both the same as and different from men. It is these inconsistencies that indicate the usefulness of a deconstructive reading – they are an indication of the way in which the attempted closure of binary oppositions has failed – and which also give us a starting point for the identification of the undecidability of the text (Gasche, 1986, p. 135). It is important to note at this point, however, that it is not being argued here that 'women' is an undecidable in the Derridean sense in Mill's text in exactly the same way it is in Locke's *Two Treatises*. Although the term is used inconsistently, it does not work in *The Subjection of Women* as the condition of possibility and impossibility of the public/private opposition. 'Women' in Mill's version of liberalism is not a hymen that is constitutive of this opposition as it is for Locke. Furthermore, the public/private opposition itself is quite differently drawn in a way that I shall argue later has been extremely important for feminist theory and practice.

In order to understand Mill's drawing of the liberal public/private opposition and women's position in relation to it we need to look at both *On Liberty* and *The Subjection of Women*. The two texts are closely related: *The Subjection of Women* may be described as an application of the principle which is set out and defended in *On Liberty* as that which should guide a progressive society: 'Over himself, over his own body and mind, the individual is sovereign (Mill, 1989a, p. 13). Despite Mill's use of the masculine pronoun I shall argue that this individual is without sex; it is the abstract individual of the feminist critique of liberalism who has no body. Against the feminist argument outlined in chapter 2, that what this means in effect is that whenever it is a question of applying the universal liberal principles of liberty and equality to concrete, embodied individuals the abstract disembodied individual of liberalism actually reveals himself as male, I shall argue that Mill's individual can be either masculine or feminine. For Mill the sovereign individual is disembodied. But the crucial opposition which he tries to draw between this individual and the society in which it is to find its 'region of human liberty' (p. 15), its personal (p. 83) or private (p. 88) sphere, is made possible and also impossible by the 'public', and in 'public opinion' there are men and women, masculine and feminine. In Mill's text it is the 'public' that is an undecidable or a 'hymen' which oscillates between support for the individual against society and support for society against the individual, so enabling the opposition between them to be made, but also preventing it from being finally closed. What this means is that in Mill's text both 'women' and 'men' participate in the undecidability of 'public opinion' for and against the individual, although with very different consequences; both 'women' and 'men' can be individuals.

Mill begins *On Liberty* with a strong statement of intent. The subject of the essay is, he says, 'the nature and limits of the power which can be legitimately exercised by society over the individual' (Mill, 1989a, p. 5). His intention is to determine where this limit should be placed, 'how to make the fitting adjustment between individual independence and social control' (p. 9). He is attempting to draw a strict opposition between the individual and society. This subject he sees as of the utmost importance since the individual is currently in great 'danger' from society: 'society has now fairly got the better of individuality (p. 61) and this is an 'evil', both for society and for the individual (p. 57). Individuality allows for the 'varieties of character' and 'experiments of living' that enable society to progress beyond its present state and it is also essential for the happiness of the individual that he should be able to exercise his own judgement in matters that concern him (p. 57).

The great danger for the individual from contemporary society is a result, according to Mill, of democracy or popular sovereignty (Mill, 1989a, pp. 7–8). We shall deal with the question of democracy in Mill's philosophy in more detail below, but for the moment we need only note that the danger of democracy is twofold: it lies in the laws that are passed by a popularly elected government and also in public opinion, which he sees as having a force independently of the law (p. 8).

In fact, he begins *On Liberty* by arguing that the power of public opinion over the individual is *more* dangerous than that of the law: 'it leaves fewer means of escape, penetrating much more deeply into the details of life, and enslaving the soul itself' (p. 8). The strength of public opinion is linked to democracy, according to Mill, because it means that increasingly account is taken of 'the will of the public', most especially by 'practical politicians', and because the social differences which made resistance to that will possible – differences in class, neighbourhoods, professions, and so on – are being eroded as general conditions, education, communication and so on are improved for all (p. 73). Initially, then, in *On Liberty*, public opinion is posited as most dangerous for the individual, as more dangerous than the law. It is to public opinion that the sphere of freedom of the individual must be opposed:

> There is a limit to the legitimate interference of collective opinion with individual independence: and to find that limit, and maintain it against encroachment, is as indispensable to a good condition of human affairs, as protection against political despotism.'
>
> (Mill, 1989a, pp. 8–9)

Almost immediately, however, Mill runs into problems with the opposition he wants to make between the individual and society. How is it to be maintained? He sets out the principle by which 'the dealings of society with the individual' are to be governed, whether it is a matter of legal penalties or 'the moral coercion of public opinion':

> That principle is, that the sole end for which mankind are warranted, individually or collectively, in interfering with the liberty of action of any of their number, is self-protection.
>
> (Mill, 1989a, p. 13)

But how is this principle to be effective? How can it be used to maintain a separation between the individual and society if public opinion – which is on the side of society and oppressive of individuality – is everywhere, leaving no means of escape, penetrating every detail of life and 'enslaving the soul itself'? (Mill, 1989a, p. 8).

Mill faces this question directly. The forces against individuality are, he argues, formidable – 'it is not easy to see how it can stand its ground' (p. 73). It may be that it will not be able to do so: It will do so with increasing difficulty, unless the intelligent part of the public can be made to feel its value – to see that it is good there should be differences . . .' (p. 73). Here we have the claim that the opposition between society and the individual can be made only if it is supported by the public, or at least by part of it. Individuality is not threatened by the public in this instance, it is sustained by it. In this sense, society cannot simply be opposed to the individual in the definitive way Mill initially intends because the public, which is on the side of society opposing the individual, is also necessary to the opposition of the individual to society; it is on the side of society and also on the side of the individual, as it were. In Derridean terms the 'public' is a hymen which is both 'society' and 'individual'; by its play between 'identity' and 'difference', between the inside and the outside, it makes possible the opposition between the society and the individual as two rigorously separated, self-identical categories at the same time as it makes the opposition between them impossible to maintain.

In order to see how the play of 'public' between individual and society makes the opposition between them both possible and impossible in Mill's text we need to look more closely at how he uses the term. In the first place, as we have seen, he uses it in strict opposition to the individual. In this sense 'the public' is one, unified against the individual:

> The . . . tendencies of the times cause the public to be more disposed than at former periods to prescribe general rules of conduct, and endeavour to make everyone conform to the approved standard.
>
> (Mill, 1989a, p. 69)

In a second usage, however, the public is not unified; it may *include* different individuals within it. It is in this sense that Mill uses it to oppose the individual to society from the side of the individual. He says that the forces hostile to individuality can only be opposed if:

> the intelligent part of the public can be made to feel its value – to see that it is good there should be differences. . . . If the claims of Individuality are ever to be asserted, the time is now, while much is still wanting to complete the enforced assimilation. . . . The demand that all other people shall resemble ourselves grows by what it feeds on. If resistance waits till life is reduced *nearly* to one uniform type, all deviations from that type will come to be considered impious, immoral, even monstrous and contrary to nature. Mankind speedily become unable to conceive diversity, when they have been for some time unable to see it.
>
> (Mill, 1989a, pp. 73–4)

In this use of 'public', then, individuals are not separate from it, opposed to it as they are to society. They are part of the public, included within it; the public includes the individuals which it opposes to society.

It is in this second sense of 'public' that Mill uses the term when he proposes in *The Subjection of Women* that the individuality of women in the private domestic sphere can be supported by public opinion. Here he uses public opinion on the side of the individual and opposes it to the law which, in this instance, stands for society against the individual. The point he wants to make is that freeing women as individuals will not lead to irreconcilable conflict in the household. Interestingly, he is here addressing Locke's problem: there must be one authority in the private domestic sphere as in the public:

> But how, it will be asked, can any society exist without government? In a family, as in a state, some one person must be the ultimate ruler. Who shall decide when married people differ in opinion? Both cannot have their way, yet a decision one way or the other must be come to.
>
> (Mill, 1989b, p. 155)

Mill's answer to this problem is, however, very different from Locke's because his concerns are different. Like Locke he wants to make a strict opposition between public and private, but the terms of the opposition are different in each case. While Locke was concerned to guarantee the self-identity of authority in the private domestic sphere as distinct from authority in the public sphere, for Mill it is the self-identity of the individual in opposition to society that is at stake.

For Mill the crucial opposition is between the private as the 'private life' of the individual (Mill, 1989a, p. 16) and the public as 'public opinion in the State' (p. 73), that is in the law made by government according to the demands of the people, or as a power in itself (p. 12). The individual in this case is genuinely unsexed as it was not for Locke. As we have seen, for Locke the free and equal human individual is both unsexed – 'human' includes both men and women – and masculine: ultimately he decides that women are women, subordinate to men, not free and equal human individuals. Women *as* women cannot, on Locke's account, be free and equal individuals. It is the principle object of *The Subjection of Women* to argue that women *are* individuals and that women's capacity for individuality is especially restricted in contemporary society. Women, Mill says, are not permitted the private happiness . . . [of] a life of rational freedom . . . the freedom of action of the individual – the liberty of each to govern his conduct by his own feelings of duty, and by such laws and social restraints as his own conscience can subscribe to.

(Mill, 1989b, p. 212)

If men's individuality is restricted in contemporary society, women's is even more so: 'social institutions do not admit the same free development of originality in women which is possible in men' (p. 143).

How, then, does Mill deal with the problem of conflict in the domestic sphere and how is it to be settled? Clearly he cannot, as Locke does, assert the natural subordination of wives to husbands in the private domestic sphere. Mill deals with it by arguing that it is not actually a real problem because 'by general custom' there is a division of labour in the home which is such that each will have their tasks and will make the decisions needed accordingly: each will be 'absolute in the executive branch of their own department' and any overall change 'of system and principle' will require the consent of both (Mill, 1989b, p. 156). Here Mill uses public opinion as supportive of the individual in opposition to law which stands for society. He argues that the division of labour between the sexes must not be established by law since that would pre-empt the freedom of the individual to live according to their own 'capacities and suitabilities' (p. 156). But it is acceptable to him that a traditional or customary division of labour should be maintained by public opinion:

When the support of the family depends, not on property, but on earnings, the common arrangement, by which the man earns the income and the wife superintends the domestic expenditure, seems to me in general the most suitable division of labour between two persons. . . . But the utmost latitude ought to exist for the adaptation of general rules to individual suitabilities; and there ought to be nothing to prevent faculties exceptionally adapted to any other pursuit, from obeying their vocation notwithstanding marriage: due provision being made for supplying otherwise any falling-short which might become inevitable, in her full performance of the ordinary functions of mistress of a family. These things, if once opinion were rightly directed on the subject, might with perfect safety be left to be regulated by opinion, without any interference of law.

(Mill, 1989b, pp. 164–5)

In this case opinion is no longer on the side of society opposed to the individual; it is on the side of the individual and opposed to the law which is now seen as dangerous in the way that public opinion was in *On Liberty*.

It is perhaps important to note here that Mill is not *a priori* opposed to the law intervening in the domestic sphere; he does not hold that the domestic sphere should be private as opposed to public in the sense that it should necessarily be outside the sphere of the law. On the contrary, he specifically argues against this view, which was widely held at the time: 'liberty is often granted where it should be withheld, as well as withheld where it should be granted' (p. 104). Husbands and fathers, he argues, do not exercise liberty in the home but power, and the state is bound to intervene to protect the rights of wives and children where necessary for their individual freedom (pp. 104–5). Nevertheless, in the case of the domestic division of labour, individual freedom is seen as possible so long as the law is absent; the 'tyranny of the prevailing opinion and feeling' that elsewhere Mill sees as especially damaging to women's individuality (p. 8) is here replaced by a public opinion which is supportive of that individuality against the state.

Public opinion is, then, an undecidable in Mill's text. Sometimes it is used on the side of society opposed to the individual; sometimes it is used on the side of the individual, to support it against society as it is represented in the law. Most notably from our point of view here, public opinion supports a division of labour which allows for individuality but which also marks a difference between men and women. The individual is unsexed for Mill, but in the public opinion which supports it in the domestic division of labour it is not. On the contrary, Mill's use of public opinion, as we have seen, distinguishes 'duties and functions' for the sexes that will permit them to complement each other, to live together without conflict. In this respect public opinion distinguishes between men and women, masculine and feminine. It is here, in the public opinion that is, as we have seen, undecidable between individual and society, that the undecidability of women between unsexed individual and feminine woman in the home comes into play.

It is important to look at some of the features of Mill's feminine woman here because many of her characteristics were used in the nineteenth-century women's movement as well as by its opponents, and because they are also repeated by feminist critiques of liberalism insofar as they rely on Chodorow's and Gilligan's accounts of sexual difference. Furthermore it is important to note these characteristics because for Mill femininity did not necessarily exclude individuality and individual rights to freedom and equality, as feminist critics maintain. Although it is true that Mill privileges masculinity and the public sphere such that the paradigm case of the individual would seem to be a man exercising his judgement according to universal principles in the public sphere, and although he sees the feminine woman's qualities as produced by oppression and as potentially dangerous to the polity, insofar as both men and women are undecidable between public opinion and the individual, the feminine woman in the private sphere is as much an individual in Mill's version of liberalism as is the masculine man in the public sphere.

We will look here at three principal characteristics of femininity which would seem to be integrally tied to the domestic division of labour for Mill. First, he argues that women are more practical than men; they are better able to perceive particular cases to which general principles do or do not apply than men, who have been educated to think speculatively in a way which often leads them 'beyond the limits of real things, and the actual facts of nature' (1989b, pp. 173–5). This feminine attribute Mill does see as commendable, arguing that it may complement and correct the reasoning of speculative men (p. 175).[2] He also ties it quite closely to women's customary occupations, to their position in the home, although he does not explicitly argue it in these terms:

A woman seldom runs after an abstraction. The habitual direction of her mind to dealing with things as individuals rather than in groups, and (what is closely connected with it) her more lively interest in the present feelings of persons, which makes her consider first of all, in anything which claims to be applied to practice, in what manner persons will be affected by it – these two things make her extremely unlikely to put faith in any speculation which loses sight of individuals, and deals with things as if they existed for some imaginary entity, some mere creation of the mind, not resolvable into the feelings of living beings.

(Mill, 1989b, p. 175)

Since, according to Mill, we should not see 'the habitual direction of her mind' as a natural consequence of her sex, these feminine characteristics can have been produced only by the circumstances of women's lives, by their position in the domestic division of labour and their exclusion from other occupations. Their domestic duties involve care for the household – a care which Mill describes as requiring 'incessant vigilance, an eye which no detail escapes' (Mill, 1989b, p. 190) – and for the interests of members of the family, 'the only ones to whom they owe any duty' (p. 193).

Second, Mill characterises the feminine woman as other-regarding rather than self-regarding. And this is closely tied to the third characterisation we shall consider, that of women as less just than men. While Mill is ostensibly concerned to argue against the opinion of his time, that women's 'judgement in grave matters is warped by their sympathies and antipathies', he actually provides some good points for this case himself (Mill, 1989b, p. 193). Initially Mill argues that it is probable that women are no less often morally biased than men but that there is a difference in the direction of this bias. According to Mill,

> men are led from the course of duty and public interest by their regard for themselves, women, (not being allowed to have private interests of their own) by their regard for somebody else.
>
> (Mill, 1989b, p. 193)

Women's concern for the general good is, then, diminished because they are other-regarding, because of their feelings for those close to them, while men are unjust because they are self-regarding, because of their own personal interest. This difference arises, he argues, because women are taught that,

> the individuals connected with them are the only ones to whom they owe any duty – the only ones whose interest they are called upon to care for; while, as far as education is concerned, they are left strangers even to the elementary ideas which are presupposed in any intelligent regard for higher interests or higher moral objects.
>
> (Mill, 1989b, p. 193)

Later in the text he argues much more strongly that women in particular are a danger to 'public virtue', principally because of their influence on husbands:

> that disinterestedness in the general conduct of life – the devotion of the energies to purposes which hold out no promise of private advantages to the family – is very seldom encouraged or supported by women's influence.
>
> (Mill, 1989b, p. 203)

Here women are seen as particularly dangerous in contrast to men, who he says, may be more willing to sacrifice their personal interests for the sake of their consciences (pp. 205–6).

For Mill, the feminine characteristics of being more other-regarding than self-regarding and tending more towards injustice than men are not natural; they are the result of circumstances and therefore relatively easy to change. He thinks that educating women, allowing them to choose their occupations and extending the franchise to allow them to participate in selecting the government, would mean that women would gain a greatly expanded sense of justice. The development of women's 'unselfish public spirit' (Mill, 1989b, p. 213) depends on the opportunities they are given to exercise their 'rational freedom' (p. 212) as human individuals:

> The mere getting rid of the idea that all the wider subjects of thought and action, all things which are of general and not solely of private interest, are men's business, from which women are to be warned off . . . the mere consciousness a woman would then have of being a human being like any other, entitled to choose her pursuits, urged or invited by the same inducements as any one else to interest herself in whatever is interesting to all human beings, entitled to exert the share of influence on all human concerns which belongs to an individual opinion, whether she attempted participation in them or not – this alone would effect an immense expansion of the faculties of women, as well as enlargement of the range of their moral sentiments.
>
> (Mill, 1989b, p. 200)

As individuals, then, women are able to transcend the narrow private interests of their households and, like the best of men, to achieve a degree of public-spiritedness. Given the way in which women's feminine characteristics in the private sphere have been opposed to this public-spiritedness, the question is, however, can women achieve it *as* women? The difference he makes between men and women in terms of their propensities for justice are, he says, grounded in the current position of the sexes:

> Whoever is in the least capable of estimating the influence on the mind of the entire domestic and social position and the whole habit of a life, must easily recognise in that influence a complete explanation of nearly all the apparent differences between men and women.
>
> (Mill, 1989b, p. 192)

If, as Mill argues, public opinion 'rightly-directed' is what is to determine the positions of men and women in the ideal future, and if, as he maintains, the management of the household and the care of those in that household will therefore continue to be 'the ordinary functions of [the] mistress of a family' (Mill, 1989b, p. 165), it is to be doubted whether women can be the public-spirited individuals he hopes they will become. Since feminine characteristics are grounded in the domestic division of labour that is supported by public opinion and since they are opposed to public-spiritedness, it would seem that women must continue to be feminine women and will fail to achieve the individuality necessary to the development of a sense of the general good. As individuals women can achieve 'the unselfish public spirit' Mill sees as desirable (p. 213); as women, it would seem, they cannot.

There is, then, scope for the feminist reading of Mill as proposing a liberalism which relies on a concept of the individual which is inherently masculine. Nevertheless, this conclusion is, I would argue, unwarranted. It is not the case that for Mill 'the individual' is synonymous with the things that men do; with, for example, working outside the home, voting and reasoning according to universal principles. It is not that on Mill's scheme, rational free individuals are only to be found in the predominantly male public sphere and not in the private domestic sphere of love and care.

It is true that for Mill men are more likely to develop their individuality than women – they are more self-regarding and less constrained by the demands of others (1989b, pp. 193 and 189–91); they would seem to have more scope to exercise their individual freedom since they have more choice in their occupations and more freedom to pursue their own interests and beliefs than women in the domestic sphere (even if on Mill's account, women initially choose housewifery as an occupation); and as individuals in the public sphere they seem much more able to cultivate the public-spiritedness which seems to denote a kind of 'higher' individuality than women confined to domestic duties.

On at least two occasions, however, Mill uses the concept of the individual in ways which do not tie it to a masculine way of life in the public sphere. First, it is because he argues that women as individuals lack freedom from the power of men in the domestic sphere that he proposes to extend the law into the private domestic sphere in order to protect that freedom (Mill, 1989a, pp. 104–5). In this case, it is the rights of women in their position as *feminine* women in the domestic sphere who are also the rational and free individuals of his philosophy that are to be protected: as feminine women they may *also* be free and equal individuals. And secondly, he argues that the reform of society that is necessary in order to make it more just – not least as regards the rights of women – requires a reformed family. At present, he argues, the family is 'a school of despotism' (Mill, 1989b, p. 160) in which men learn to enjoy the power they exercise over others. Although they may adopt in principle what Mill calls 'the law of justice', that the weak should have equal right with the strong, because of the way they learn that superiority in the home is their birthright they will be working against it 'in their inmost sentiments' (pp. 196–9). According to Mill, rather than being a 'school of despotism' the family should be a 'school of the virtues of freedom' (p. 160). It should teach its members to live together according to the moral rule that should govern human society in general (1989b, p. 161):

> the true virtue of human beings is fitness to live together as equals; claiming nothing for themselves but what they as freely concede to every one else. . . . The family, justly constituted would be the real school of the virtues of freedom.
>
> (Mill, 1989b, p. 160)

It would seem that what the family should teach is the practice of living together according to Mill's first principle, as laid out in *On Liberty*: that the freedom of the individual should not be interfered with so long as his/her actions do not harm others (Mill, 1989a, p. 13). To this end, women must have equal rights in the home in order to protect their freedom as individuals, and men must restrict their authority in the home so as not to interfere with the rights of both women and children. In this case, *contra* the feminist critiques of liberalism as essentially masculinist, the individual is genuinely unsexed, it is not exclusively masculine: both feminine women and masculine men may be individuals.

In these two cases Mill's individual is in the private domestic sphere and requires an area of personal autonomy – a 'region of human liberty' (Mill, 1989a, p. 15) – around its person. In this respect the opposition Mill makes between society and the individual, between public and private, cuts across the distinction between public – state and civil society – and private domestic. The individual has a 'private life' (p. 16) inside the private domestic sphere. Given, however, that binary oppositions are necessarily unstable, the binary opposition between public and private is not definitively fixed in Mill's text. As we have seen, the opposition between individual and society, and as it depends on it, also that between women as individuals and as feminine women in the domestic division of labour, is made both possible and impossible by the operation of 'public' as a hymen. Mill's 'women' can never be definitively included in the category of 'individual', and nor can they be definitively excluded. Sometimes women, even the feminine woman who chooses to be a wife and mother in the domestic sphere, are individuals whose rights must be protected and whose freedom must be cultivated; at other times they are women whose 'duties and functions' are laid down by public opinion and whose individual freedom must be curtailed by their position in the domestic sphere.

Where women should be placed in relation to this opposition individual/feminine is a matter of an 'ethico-theoretical' decision for the reader of the text. While Pateman reads it as constructing women as confined to the private domestic sphere, and therefore as outside the terms of a liberalism which is valid only in the public sphere, it seems clear that Mill himself made the decision in favour of women as individuals. He argues for the individual against society and it is the object of *The Subjection of Women* to show how women have been unjustly subordinated to men in the private sphere through their femininity and through their exclusion from the public world of work and politics. As we shall see in the final section of this chapter, first-wave feminism was inclined not to decide at all, to leave open the undecidability of Mill's liberalism, on which it drew heavily for legitimation of its demands. Although in practice decisions had to be made between the identity of women as rational self-determining individuals and the identity of women as feminine and domestic, in general feminists were unwilling definitively to decide for one rather than the other. Before we examine the first-wave feminist use of the liberal undecidability of women, however, we must consider the other important change in liberalism in the nineteenth century, its articulation with democracy.

THE DEMOCRATISATION OF LIBERALISM AND THE LIBERALISATION OF DEMOCRACY

Mill's Articulation of Liberalism and Democracy

The relationship between liberalism and democracy is a complicated one. Insofar as democracy may be defined as rule by consent of the people it seems to have been implied by liberalism from the beginning;

it is a requirement of legitimate government for Locke that it should have the people's consent (Arblaster, 1984, p. 75). However, although he develops the rudiments of a theory of majority rule and representative government, Locke's notion of consent does not entail for him that the people should *actually* participate in the election of government or the making of laws. It is not a condition of legitimate government by consent for Locke that there should be regular periodic elections and he certainly did not envisage universal suffrage (Held, 1987, p. 54).

The limitations of Locke's notion of consent should not necessarily be seen, however, as inconsistencies in his theory; it is not that his notion of consent *logically* implies the actual participation of the people in electing a legislative and that Locke was mistaken or disingenuous about drawing out the implications of his liberalism. The notion of consent does not logically imply the need for the actual participation of the people for Locke because, as we have seen in chapter 3, for him actual empirical differences in the people to be governed, including sexual differences, are irrelevant in the framing of the laws by which they are to live. There is no need for legislators to be directly accountable to the people, far less for the people themselves to participate directly in law-making, because the criteria by which laws are to be judged as just is that they should be for the good of the people as a whole and that they should be universal. Providing they protect the 'lives, liberties and estates' of each citizen equally there is no reason why the people should *not* consent to them. For Locke, as long as the people do not actually revolt as one against its legislative, something it should do on his account if natural rights are infringed (Locke, 1960, pp. 412–13), and as long as the form of the law is universal, the consent of the governed can be assumed: the trust which the people put in government on entering civil society has not been violated and that government may be considered legitimate. In Locke's words:

These are the bounds which the trust that is put in them by the society and the law of God and Nature have set to the legislative power of every commonwealth, in all forms of government. First: They are to govern by promulgated established laws, not to be varied in particular cases, but to have one rule for rich and poor, for the favourite at Court, and the countryman at plough. Secondly: These laws also ought to be designed for no other end ultimately but the good of the people. Thirdly: They must not raise taxes on the property of the people without the consent of the people given by themselves or their deputies. . . . Fourthly: Legislative neither must

nor can transfer the power of making laws to anybody else, or place
it anywhere but where the people have.

(Locke, 1960, p. 409)

In this respect, then, Locke's liberalism conforms to that criticised
by difference feminists as masculinist. Excluding difference from the
public sphere for the sake of universality, Lockean liberalism denies
the very possibility that sexual difference could ever be represented
there. Women can only enter the public sphere insofar as they can be
subsumed in the unified category of 'the people' or 'mankind'; they
cannot appear there as women in their specificity. Women are undecidable,
in Locke's terms, as we have seen, between the generic category 'mankind' and the specific category of 'women' as subordinate in the private
sphere, but on his account there is no possibility of representing women
as women in their specific difference from men in the public sphere.

The same is not true, however, of Mill's version of liberalism. In
contrast to Locke's account of legitimate government, Mill argues that
there are significant divisions within the people, so that on his theory
the good of the whole cannot simply be assumed from the universal
form of the law and from the fact that the government has not been
explicitly rejected in revolution. In the importance he places on differences *within* the people Mill breaks with Locke's classical liberalism.

At the same time, Mill's articulation of liberalism and democracy
breaks with the democratic tradition too. Liberalism and democracy
were first linked in the works of Jeremy Bentham and James Mill, and
this represented a fundamental break with previous attempts to theorise democracy; before this it had not been thought of as possible in a
divided society (Macpherson, 1977, p. 9). Previously political theorists had tried to think democracy in terms of the identity of the governed and the governing and this required the people to be unified. For
Rousseau, for example, the sovereignty of the general will requires the
unity of the people, otherwise it cannot be an expression of the common good (p. 17). The crucial division recognised by nineteenth-century
liberal democrats was that between classes in a capitalist market society;
although Bentham and Mill did recognise other divisions, including
the division between men and women, they placed most weight on the
conflict between classes, between the rich and the poor (pp. 20–1).[3]
Although Mill also wrote sometimes as if class were the most important division in modern society (for example, Mill, 1946, pp. 187–8),
gender inequalities were crucial to his theory of liberal-democracy, as
The Subjection of Women makes clear. He also makes scattered references

to other divisions he saw as important: to inequalities based on race (Mill, 1973a, pp. 181–2), to differences of religion and political party (Mill, 1973a, p. 239), and to the danger in general in which minorities faced with majorities find themselves (Mill, 1946, pp. 183–4). It is John Stuart Mill, then, who offers the most comprehensive attempt of the nineteenth century to think the articulation of liberalism and democracy in a divided society.

Like Bentham and James Mill, J.S. Mill saw universal suffrage as inevitable (Macpherson, 1977, p. 45). And like Tocqueville, on whose analysis of democracy in America he based much of his own, he believed that the important problem was 'Not to determine whether democracy shall come, but how to make the best of it when it does come' (Mill, 1973a, pp. 174–5). The masses, he argued, had realised their strength and could not ultimately be stopped from asserting it (p. 175). In order to 'make the best of it', Mill sought, as liberals must, to limit democracy in important ways; democratic decisions may not necessarily accord with liberal principles.

As a liberal, then, Mill was suspicious of democracy, but as well as seeing it as inevitable Mill also argued that it was, for the most part, a good thing because different groups in society may have different interests. There are two parts to this argument. First, they may have different interests and therefore all should be represented:

the rights and interests of every or any person are only secure from being disregarded when the person interested is himself able, and habitually disposed, to stand up for them.

(Mill, 1946, p. 142)

But second, even if different groups do not *actually* have different interests, they will nevertheless see things from different perspectives, and each position should be represented. According to Mill it is extremely difficult for any group to recognise its 'real' interests, and what weaker groups have to protect themselves against is what those with power take their 'immediate and apparent interest' to be when it conflicts with how the weaker groups see things (Mill, 1946, p. 183). As Mill puts it:

it suffices that, in the absence of its natural defenders, the interest of the excluded is always in danger of being overlooked; and when looked at, is seen with very different eyes from those of the persons whom it directly concerns.

(p. 143)

Mill also sees democracy as a good thing because participation in the election of governments will improve the individual, making him/her less concerned with his/her private and family interests and more able to appreciate and recognise the public good. According to Mill, by voting, and by fulfilling other public functions – serving on juries and on parish councils, for example – an individual will learn 'identification with the public':

> He is called upon, while so engaged, to weigh interests not his own; to be guided, in case of conflicting claims, by another rule than his private partialities; to apply, at every turn, principles and maxims which have for their reason of existence the common good . . .
>
> (Mill, 1946, p. 150)

Those without a vote, he argues, will continue to concern themselves only with their private interests and those of their families (Mill, 1946, pp. 210–11), and this will be detrimental to the progress and prosperity of society as a whole.

Insofar, then, as he is concerned that different perspectives should be represented in the public sphere, and not confined to the private sphere as Locke's version of liberalism would have it, Mill's liberal democratic theory does not necessarily result in the exclusion of women's specific concerns from the realm of public consideration. For Mill, in contradistinction to Locke, and to the feminist characterisation of liberalism as masculinist, the public sphere is not the sphere of universality but of conflicting perspectives, which must each be represented there for the sake of justice and the protection of different interests and also for the sake of the development of a sense of the common good on the part of each individual.

Mill argues for the extension of the franchise to women for both these reasons. First, because women's interests may differ significantly from men's, though he does not anticipate that they will always do so:

> The majority of the women of any class are not likely to differ in political opinion from the majority of men of the same class, unless the question be one in which the interests of women, as such, are in some way involved; and if they are so, women require the suffrage, as their guarantee of just and equal consideration.
>
> (Mill, 1989b, p. 169)

Second, Mill argues that granting the vote to women will have an 'ennobling influence', which will draw them out of the narrow interests of their circumscribed lives in the private sphere and contribute to the development of a more 'unselfish public spirit' (p. 213).

For Mill it is precisely *because* women are, or may be, different from men that they must be represented in the public sphere. This is not to say, of course, that given the means of representation it then follows that women will necessarily represent themselves as different from men. On the contrary, Mill leaves the question of how women will represent themselves open: in class terms, as like men, or as women with their own specific concerns. Nevertheless, insofar as he believes that there is a 'common good' with which the public spirited citizen will identify, he does preclude the possibility that women will represent themselves as having interests that are irrevocably in conflict with those of men. In this respect he does foreclose the possibility of a radical and irreconcilable difference of perceived interest between the sexes.

Mill's notion of the common good is, I would argue, indicative of a more general failure on his part to think through the implications of his articulation of liberalism and democracy; he does not fully follow through the consequences of his own argument that politics is a matter of competing perspectives. If, as he argues, individuals are to be the final arbitrators of their own interests and if there are fundamental differences in society which make the representation of those interests necessary, there would seem to be no *a priori* reason why there should be a 'common good' at all, far less one which all parties would recognise as such. Mill does not consider the possibility that there might be irreconcilable conflicts between perspectives which could not be resolved into a higher synthesis. It may be that his argument is internally consistent because he tacitly assumes, though he does not explicitly thematise it, a typically nineteenth century teleological theory of social development in which harmony is assured by the direction of progress (Bellamy, 1992, p. 24). However, if we reject such an implied teleology as untenable, the anomalies of Mill's position become clear.

Hegemonic Liberal-democracy

The characteristics of democracy Mill's philosophy implies but does not explicitly thematise are elucidated by considering it from the point of view of Claude Lefort's theory of democracy outlined in the previous chapter. It clearly shows the implications of democracy as a form of politics involving competing perspectives, without any necessary resolution, for modern social and political institutions.

As we have seen, democracy in Lefort's sense of the term, is a condition of permanent instability which, following Laclau and Mouffe, can only ever be temporarily and contingently fixed in particular forms by successful hegemonic projects (Laclau and Mouffe, 1985, pp. 186–9). Hegemonic projects are only possible where there is democracy in this sense, and liberal democracy is only possible where a successful hegemonic project ensures the institutions that make it possible; it is only possible when the social has been fixed into certain forms.

In Britain, Mill was, of course, one of the chief theorists of the forms of liberal democracy during the period in which their social foundations were being laid down. But Lefort's analysis of the democratic revolution as instituting the possibility of irresolvable contestation goes beyond democracy as Mill sees it, as the institutional procedures that are needed to ensure the representation of conflicting perspectives in modern societies. It does imply the necessity Mill sees for these procedures but, as John Thompson argues, it is a theory of the way in which society was instituted in a new form in modernity, rather than of a specific institution or set of institutions (editor's introduction to Lefort, 1986, p. 20).

Lefort's analysis clearly brings out, then, the implications of Mill's argument that there is a plurality of perspectives in modern society which must be represented. Following the democratic revolution, on Lefort's account, there can be no guarantee of the common good such as Mill hoped for or anticipated; there can be no necessary progress towards a higher state of society, but only conflict between perspectives which can never be finally resolved. For Lefort, not only are there always different perspectives that must be represented in the public sphere, as Mill argued, but more importantly, the terms of liberal democracy itself are also open to contestation. Lefort's concept of *le politique* as the contestation and articulation of the symbolic which enables the institution of new social forms goes beyond the narrow definition of the politics of liberal-democratic institutions, *la politique*: it is in *le politique* that the very terms of *la politique*, the terms with which are concerned in this study – the oppositions between public and private, between masculinity and femininity, between women as individuals or constrained by the duties of their femininity and as different from or the same as men – are defined, articulated and contested in attempts to institute new social and political practices.

Furthermore, Lefort's theorisation of the egalitarian potential of modernity, also brings out another feature of Mill's articulation of liberalism and democracy: democracy is the extension of rights. Mill's theory of liberal democracy is primarily a recognition of *political* rights, the right to representative government. But, beyond this, it is also the institutionalisation of conflicts concerning rights which cannot be confined to the level of *la politique*. In Lefort's view, rights are never *merely* formal, they cannot be contained at the level of liberal political and legal rights since once the 'right to have rights' is instituted it can be used to articulate demands for equality and freedom from oppression across the social (Lefort, 1986, ch. 7). In the case we are interested in here, rights can be used to legitimate women's demands for equality and freedom in the private domestic sphere as well as the public sphere. Although Mill's articulation of liberalism and democracy limits, and is intended to limit, the scope of democracy as it had been attempted in the French Revolution – by making it representative rather than direct, popular democracy and by restricting its scope to the public sphere – at the same time it points beyond itself to the wider sense of democracy as potentially challenging of *all* forms of inequality and oppression.

Two possible objections to Lefort's thesis need to be considered at this point. First, although Lefort has been influenced by Tocqueville's analysis of democracy as an 'irreversible dynamic', in which equality in the political sphere seems to lead more or less inevitably to equality in other areas of the social (Lefort, 1988, p. 14), Lefort does not himself argue that the extension of rights is *automatic* following the French Revolution, that there is something in rights themselves that prompts their outward expansion. This kind of teleological account would be at odds with both Lefort's own account of democracy as contestation and with the resistance and reversals to which rights demands have actually been subject historically. What Lefort maintains is that rights are effective insofar as they are used to contest relations of subordination and to institute new relations based on the acceptance of a greater degree of equality and freedom:

> These rights are one of the generative principles of democracy . . . Their effectiveness stems from the allegiance that is given them, and this allegiance is bound up with a way of being in society, which cannot be measured by the mere preservation of acquired benefits. In short, rights can not be disassociated from the awareness of rights: this is my first observation. But it is no less true that this awareness of rights is all the more widespread when they are declared, when power is said to guarantee them, when liberties are made visible by laws. Thus the awareness of right and its institutionalisation are ambiguously related.
>
> (Lefort, 1986, p. 260)

Second, it is perhaps open to question the extent to which demands for greater equality have been made in terms of *rights* in Britain, where the history of democracy has been so different from that of France (Arblaster, 1987, pp. 41–5). This is a difficult question to assess. Is it only demands made specifically in terms of human rights to liberty and equality, and only insofar as they are instituted in the name of these rights, that can count as 'democratic' in Lefort's terms? Or is it rather that all demands which aim generally at greater freedom and equality, even if they are not couched in terms of rights and even if they are instituted for pragmatic reasons rather than on the basis of a stated recognition of their legitimacy, may be considered as democratic? Certainly in the case of Britain the second kind of demand has been much more common than the first. Mill's arguments against women's subordination were based on utility not rights, though to the extent that he argues for freedom and equality for women on the grounds of their own happiness as self-determining individuals, rather than the good of society or the progress of humanity, he does come very close to a natural rights argument (Coole, 1988, pp. 115–17; Charvet, 1982, pp. 33–4). And, as we shall see, feminist campaigns in the nineteenth century were based on a range of arguments, including rights-claims, pragmatism and a kind of utilitarianism (in the form of the claim that women's participation in politics would improve the morality of society generally), while on at least one occasion the institution of these demands in law was made in terms which explicitly rejected a formulation in terms of equality between the sexes (Shanley, 1989, p. 70). It seems reasonable, however, to see first-wave feminist campaigns, and to the extent that they were successful, the institution of the demands they made, as democratic in Lefort's terms insofar as they broadly involved the claim that there should be a greater degree of equality, if not absolute equality, between the sexes, and that women should have the protection of the law against abuse by men, so increasing their personal freedom. Though feminist demands were often not explicitly made, nor instituted, in terms of rights, they nevertheless aimed at, and to some extent achieved, a greater degree of sexual equality than had previously been the case and a greater degree of freedom for women. In this respect it is reasonable to see them as demanding, and to some extent, instituting democratic rights for women.

FIRST-WAVE FEMINISM: COUNTER-HEGEMONIC LIBERALISM

Until quite recently historians of first-wave feminism tended to portray it as representing women in two principal lines of argument, both of which may be seen as challenging the public/private opposition of classical liberalism in different ways: the first relies on liberal rights to equality and liberty on the grounds of the common humanity of men and women to argue for legal and educational and occupational reform, the second on extending women's specifically feminine influence into the public sphere through social reform and woman's suffrage. Following Aileen Kraditor's influential work on the women's movement in nineteenth-century and early twentieth-century North America there was a tendency to see these arguments as sequential. Early first-wave feminists, Kraditor maintained, argued for the vote on the grounds of natural rights to equality, referring to the Declaration of the Rights of Man and extending it to women on the grounds of common humanity; but later they shifted the grounds of their claims to the *difference* between men and women, demanding the vote for the protection of women's interests and, most significantly, because women's influence could be used to bring about needed social and moral reform (Kraditor, 1981, pp. 45–52). According to Kraditor, feminist arguments for the vote shifted from demands for justice to claims based on women's special qualities at the moment when the rights of the governed to consent to government were being called into question by white men in relation to the poor of the expanding cities and to new immigrants. The change in the grounds of feminist arguments was therefore associated with a shift from radicalism to expediency, an expediency which was conservative and racist since it confirmed women's essential femininity and explicitly excluded the working class and immigrants from voting (Kraditor, 1981, ch. 7). A similar shift, though possibly less marked and less overtly racist because of the different social context, was noted in Britain by Olive Banks:

> As feminism grew in influence and became, in the great suffrage campaign of the early twentieth century, something of a mass movement, it shed not only its more radical goals but its more radical conception of womanhood. . . . By the end of the nineteenth century, the feminist movement was based, not so much on the doctrine of male and female equality as on a notion of female superiority that was accepted not only by women but by many of their male supporters.
>
> (Banks, 1981, p. 85)

Feminine superiority, Banks suggests, was a more acceptable basis than equality between the sexes from which to argue for the extension of women's influence via the vote because it was less damaging to conservative opinion (p. 98). Banks goes so far as to argue that by the end of the nineteenth century there is such a contradiction between definitions of women as, on the one hand essentially the same as men, and on the other as essentially different, that there is not one feminism, but two, facing in completely opposite directions (p. 102).

For these historians of first-wave feminism, then, it was equal rights arguments that were radical, while arguments from difference were seen as inherently conservative. Recently, however, in sympathy with the disillusion with equal rights arguments that also informs the feminist critique of liberalism as masculinist, historians have taken issue with this portrayal of first-wave feminism as fundamentally divided between liberalism and conservatism and have constructed a more complex understanding of the movement (Bacchi, 1990, pp. 97–101). According to revisionists the 'two faces' version of first-wave feminism neglects the extent to which arguments based on women's moral superiority were made by so-called liberal feminists in the early years of the movement (Rendall, 1987) and also the extent to which, although there was a shift in emphasis, arguments continued to be made on the basis of women's rights as liberal individuals into the twentieth century (Bacchi, 1990, ch. 1; Holton, 1986, pp. 11–18). Furthermore, it is generally agreed that, although historians may have been puzzled by their inconsistency, few first-wave feminists saw it as contradictory to argue for women's difference and superiority to men while at the same time claiming equal rights to participation in 'male' institutions (Bacchi, 1990, pp. 22–3). One way to understand this apparently unproblematic inconsistency is to relate it to the undecidability of women in liberalism itself, between women as individuals, free and equal and indistinguishable from men, and women as feminine with specific functions and characteristics. It is an inconsistency within liberalism itself, and not just between liberalism and other perspectives, more conservative on the older reading and possibly more radical from the perspective of 'difference' feminists.

It is true that, arguing from a liberal point of view, John Stuart Mill himself was hostile to the use of 'difference' arguments. An article, probably co-authored with Harriet Taylor, which noted this tendency in American feminism condemned

> those who would meekly attempt to combine nominal equality between men and women, with enforced distinctions in their privileges

and functions. What is wanted for women is equal rights, equal admission to all social privileges; not a position apart, a sort of senti-
mental priesthood. . . . The strength of the cause lies in the support
of those who are influenced by reason and principle; and to attempt
to recommend it by sentimentalities, absurd in reason, and inconsistent with the principle on which the movement is founded, is to
place a good cause on a level with a bad one.

(quoted in Holton, 1986, pp. 11–12)

But as we have seen, Mill's articulation of women's rights along strictly
liberal principles of abstract individualism relied on, and so was not
able finally to exclude, the possibility of feminine difference. Feminists, in oscillating between arguments based on sameness and on difference, may be seen as using the undecidability inherent in liberalism's
own positioning of women. They did not confine themselves to liberalism's 'official' doctrine of the interchangeability of abstract individuals
governed by universal principles, but developed this alongside its cov-
ert doctrine of women's specificity as women. Furthermore, Mill's articulation of liberalism and democracy explicitly asserted women's
difference. As we have seen, on Mill's account, it was because women
might have a different perspective from men and different interests, as
well as being in special need of developing a wider sense of the public good than was available to them so long as they were confined to
the private sphere, that they needed representation in government. Though
Mill himself might have disagreed with arguments for women's influence in the public sphere on the basis of their moral superiority, such
arguments are fully consistent with his own formulation of liberal-
democracy.

Seen until recently, then, as confusingly split between equal rights
arguments and arguments from women's moral superiority, the complexity of first-wave feminism is now much better appreciated. It drew
on several different influences: liberalism was the most important but
the evangelical Christianity that contributed to the cult of domesticity
was also significant and so too, though much less prominently, were
socialist ideals of co-operativity (Banks, 1981, pp. 7–8; Garner, 1984,
pp. 2–3).[4] Without wanting to deny this complexity, the focus here is
on the relationship between feminism and liberalism, so that it is to
this relationship as it was worked out in specific feminist campaigns
that we shall direct our attention. We shall look at the way in which
first-wave feminism used liberalism against itself, or more precisely at
the way in which it used Mill's liberal and democratic arguments for

equal rights in private and public spheres, against the classical liberal positioning of women as ultimately subordinate to men in the private domestic sphere. The arguments used are generally recognisably derived from Mill's writings, and indeed *The Subjection of Women* has been described as the 'bible of the women's movement in Anglo-Saxon countries' (Bacchi, 1990, pp. 7–8). However, the feminist counter-hegemonic use of liberalism also went beyond 'official' liberalism insofar as it used both possibilities of Mill's undecidability, oscillating between the construction of women as abstract individuals and as feminine, and specifically maternal, women. We shall also look at this aspect of the use of 'unofficial' liberalism.

First-wave feminism was also enormously complex insofar as it spanned three-quarters of a century – from the 1850s to the 1920s or 1930s – and encompassed campaigns directed at almost every aspect of women's lives. Here again we will have to simplify and direct our attention to three campaigns which will be used to illustrate the feminist contestation of women's position in the private sphere and of the public/private opposition itself: the campaign for the legal reform of marriage which drew on universal liberal principles of liberty and equality and applied them in the private domestic sphere; the extension of domesticity and of women's special qualities into the conventionally conceived public sphere in campaigns for social reform which also drew on rights claims; and the campaign for the vote which came to symbolise women's claims both to self-determination and equality with men and also to a recognition of women's specific value *as* women.[5]

It is uncontroversial to argue that the legal reform of relations between the sexes in the private domestic sphere should be counted as a relatively successful application of liberal principles of freedom and equality where they had previously been excluded as inapplicable.[6] As we have seen, women in the private sphere were undecidable for Locke between individuals who contracted into marriage on a equal basis with men and who had, therefore, the right to negotiate terms and break the contract, and women who were naturally subordinate to their husbands. In practice, however, in the eighteenth and nineteenth centuries the law of coverture meant that a woman gave up practically all rights on marriage: she could not sue or be sued, sign contracts without her husband's signature accompanying hers, own real property outright or secure personal property for her own use. Nor could a woman easily obtain a divorce, while if she separated from her husband she still had no rights to her own income nor to the custody of her children (Shanley, 1989, pp. 8–9). From the beginning of organised feminism in the 1850s this form of marriage was under attack as inhumane and as contravening accepted liberal principles of justice (Banks, 1981, p. 10). In a series of Acts passed in the second half of the nineteenth century feminists succeeded in gaining legal rights for women to hold property in their own names, to appeal for custody of their children and to sue for separation from abusive husbands (Shanley, 1989, p. 14). Using Mill's version of liberalism in which women were to be positioned as individuals in the private domestic sphere – a possibility that could not be entirely excluded by Locke, but which he decided against and which was excluded in legal practice – feminists challenged the liberal opposition between the public sphere of universal principles of liberty and equality and the private sphere of natural inequality and subordination. As Mary Shanley puts it:

> In their campaigns, feminists relied heavily on the liberal principles of individual autonomy and equality to persuade Parliament to end the legal subordination of married women. In the process they used liberal theory itself to demolish the traditional distinction between the 'public' world of politics and the 'private' world of the family.
> (Shanley, 1989, p. 20)

The reservations concerning the success of this feminist use of liberal principles are first, the criticism that is invariably made of liberalism from the left and from second-wave feminists, that it only makes changes at the level of formal political and legal rights and fails to take into account social and economic inequalities which render them meaningless (Mitchell, 1987). It is true that early feminists neglected the unequal access of married women to participation in the paid economy and they accepted the conventional household division of labour, as Mill did, though they actively campaigned for occupations for unmarried women and for celibacy as a valid way of life. But the reforms they proposed did specifically address the injustice of married women's economic and social inequality. The Married Women's Property Acts that were passed obviously dealt with economic inequality, and not only that of middle-class married women. The Act of 1870, for example, was argued for and conceded in parliament on the grounds that while rich women could safeguard real property in trust, poorer women were not able to secure even their own earnings from unscrupulous husbands (Shanley, 1989, p. 70). And in social terms the campaign for legal rights must be seen as part of the wider feminist struggle which aimed at gaining respect for women as equals, both in marriage and outside it (Shanley, 1989, pp. 66–7; Levine, 1990, p. 108). Their success in this respect is extremely difficult to assess, but insofar as the law has a symbolic effect on social relations which fall outside the scope of its application (O'Donovan, 1985, pp. 19–20), and insofar as campaigns aimed at changing the law necessarily raise public consciousness, liberal rights, even of the most limited kind, must be seen as valuable tools of social transformation. We shall return to the question of the limitations of liberalism in this respect in the following chapter.

Second, nineteenth-century feminist reforms of the private domestic sphere may be seen as only partially successful, not simply because they failed fully to institute the changes aimed for (the details of which we cannot go into here – see Shanley, 1989), but because they failed to gain official acceptance of the liberal principle that men and women are equal. Though passing broadly gender-neutral laws, parliament repeatedly refused to concede the principle of the equality of the sexes. To take the Married Women's Property Act of 1870 as an example again, the original Bill, which stated that the common law with respect to married women's property was 'unjust in principle', was amended to state only that 'it is desirable to amend the law of property and contract with respect to married women' (Shanley, 1989, p. 71). This followed parliamentary debate in which it was argued that the law was not unjust because 'the wife was the weaker vessel, . . . there ought to be only one head of the house, and . . . the husband was the proper head' (p. 70). In other words, the law was passed for pragmatic reasons and failed to institute the liberal principle of universal equality as valid in the private domestic sphere. With regard to Lefort's argument that democratic rights are extended on the basis of their acceptance and institution this would seem to be a serious reservation concerning the effectiveness of these reforms. At the same time, however, it also seems to be indicative of a sense of the power of even the most basic of legal rights – of what would be called formal rights by critics – to subvert existing social relations. Defenders of the status quo had a highly developed sense of the danger of claims feminists were making to liberal rights in the private domestic sphere of the household, and this suggests that the degree of liberty and equality feminists undoubtedly did win for women in the nineteenth century should not be seen as negligible. Even if it was not officially recognised as such, it would seem to represent a significant concession to liberal principles and an improvement in women's rights on which future feminists could build.

It is also uncontroversial that women used the value of femininity as it had been constructed in the cult of domesticity to extend their influence into what was conventionally thought of as the public sphere. Justified by the argument that women were inherently maternal and caring, spiritual and wise, women moved – quite forcefully in the face of the hostility of male governors and managers – into newly established charitable institutions and the home visiting that was the prototype of social work (Summers, 1979; Prochaska, 1980). They were able to do so without contradicting their definition of women as essentially maternal, and so influential in the private sphere, because they offered a view of the home that was similar to that of the cult of domesticity – it was the place of love and care which guaranteed the moral order of society – but with the difference that it was seen as an active social agency rather than as a place of retreat. As such Josephine Butler argued for

> the extension beyond our homes of the home influence . . . nothing whatever will avail but the infusion of Home elements into Workhouses, Hospitals, Schools, Orphanages, Lunatic Asylums, Reformatories, and even Prison.
>
> (quoted in Holton, 1986, p. 14)

Interestingly, this type of argument could be couched in terms of women's *rights* to care. Florence Hill pushed for admission to institutions on the grounds that:

> 'woman's mission' is to tend the young, and nurse the sick, is a proposition constantly urged by the opposite sex, and fully accepted by her own. That 'woman's rights' involve therefore her admission on at least equal terms to the management of institutions whereof the inmates consist chiefly of those two classes, would appear to be a necessary deduction from that proposition.
>
> (quoted in Prochaska, 1980, p. 143)

This aspect of first-wave feminism is, however, generally seen as derived from evangelical Christianity rather than liberalism, and is sometimes seen as explicitly contradicting the humanist premises on which liberal principles of liberty and equality are founded (Banks, 1981, p. 84). While religion was certainly an important resource both for the construction of the cult of domesticity and the feminist use of the hegemonic ideal of women's superior moral nature, and while arguments from women's special nature *as* women and liberal feminist arguments based on the common humanity of the pre-social individual may *logically* be mutually exclusive, the undecidability in nineteenth-century liberalism itself, between women as women with specific duties and functions and women as individuals and therefore possessing rights, allows for the oscillation between, and sometimes the combination of, these two possibilities. In other words, arguments from women's special nature do not deny or contradict liberal arguments because women's specificity was not completely excluded – and has never been completely excluded – by liberal theory. Feminists using maternalist arguments are more usefully seen, then, as extending values associated with women and the private sphere *in liberal theory and practice itself* as they coexist in tension with the more inclusive principles of individual liberty and equality. The deconstructive reading of liberalism as dependent on constitutive undecidability allows us to understand something which puzzles those for whom the 'two faces of feminism' are mutually exclusive: how it was that from the very beginning of organised feminism, intelligent and highly aware women could argue from both positions. Comparing the views of Josephine Butler, prominent in social and moral reform throughout the second half of the nineteenth century, with those of a member of the Langham Place circle, explicitly set up for legal, political and economic reform and connected with the progressive liberal establishment, including Mill himself, Olive Banks noted that:

> if it is no surprise that Josephine Butler believed in the special and redemptive mission of women, it is perhaps more unexpected to find Mrs Jameson, one of the Langham Place circle, writing in 1852 of the 'coming moral regeneration and complete harmonious development in the whole human race through the feminine element in society'.
>
> (Banks, 1981, pp. 89–90)

In fact, the apparently inconsistent arguments of this group – the mixture of articles and arguments asserting the need to carry private values into the public sphere which accompanied the expression of conventionally understood liberal political and economic claims in the journal associated with it in its early days (Rendall, 1987, pp. 137–8) – become comprehensible once we take the undecidability of liberalism itself into account. While some, Mill amongst them, were anxious to contain what is sometimes called social maternalism in the name of liberal universality, for the feminist movement in general there was no need to make a final decision between the two. As we have seen, the notion of women's specificity coexisted in tension with universalist humanism in Mill's version of liberalism (as in Locke's and in subsequent versions too) and for many liberal feminists in the nineteenth century they coexisted in feminist theory and practice too.

Arguments drawing on women's moral superiority were extensively used in the campaign for female suffrage. This campaign was itself an immensely complex, long drawn out affair, beginning in the mid-nineteenth century and growing into a mass movement which dominated feminism by the early twentieth century.[7] Within this movement there were various groups, including some of the social welfarists referred to above and members of the labour movement as well as the Liberal feminists and suffragettes traditionally associated with demands for the vote (Holton, 1986, pp. 1–8; Banks, 1981, pp. 121–4). These groups all had different concerns, but for all of them the vote became a crucial symbol of the possibility of change in women's position in public and private spheres (Bryson, 1992, p. 87). It is likely that the increased emphasis given to women's specific moral qualities was a way of uniting disparate groups who came to see themselves, to a greater or lesser extent, as set apart from the men with whom they were otherwise associated, as a 'sex-class' (Holton, 1986, p. 7).[8] Increasingly it was on the basis of women's difference from men rather than on the basis of equal rights with men, though such arguments continued to feature in the suffrage campaign and afterwards, that the vote was demanded (Holton, 1986, ch. 1).

Arguments on the grounds that women needed the vote because of their difference from men were not only consistent with the 'unofficial' doctrine of women's specificity in liberalism, they were actually made explicit in Mill's articulation of liberalism and democracy. According to Mill, women needed the vote in order to protect their perceived interests, as well as for their development as rational self-determining individuals, precisely because they had, or might have, different interests from the men who were supposed, according to traditional views, to represent them. Democracy on Mill's account involved the representation of different perspectives and so it went beyond Locke's ideal of justice in politics as the framing of universal laws. It also, as I have argued, although Mill did not recognise it, went beyond the utilitarian ideal of the common good. Arguing for representation on the grounds of women's specificity was not, then, in contradiction with liberal-democracy because, in Mill's terms, liberal-democracy involved more than the equal participation of self-determining individuals in government; it actually required different perspectives, different perceptions of interest in order to be realised.[9]

That women had different interests from men was not in dispute for suffragists. As Millicent Fawcett, leader of the largest organised group in the suffrage movement put it:

> If men and women were exactly alike, the representation of men would represent us; but not being alike, that wherein we differ is unrepresented under the present system.
>
> (M. Fawcett, in Lewis, 1979, p. 419)

However, feminists went beyond what Mill anticipated, or could support, when they argued that women's maternal influence would have an improving effect on politics and on morality and would particularly contribute to the areas with which the state was newly concerned: the education of children, public health, and the management and care of the poor (Holton, 1986, p. 11). To quote Fawcett again:

> We do not want women to be bad imitations of men; we neither deny nor minimise the differences between men and women. The claim of women to representation depends to a large extent on these differences. Women bring something to the service of the state different to that which can be brought by men.
>
> (quoted in Holton, 1986, p. 12)

Not all feminists agreed with the definition of women as morally superior or as having particularly maternal characteristics; for some too much had been made of sexual difference and women and men were above all similar as human beings (Kent, 1990, p. 207). All suffragists, however, expected to use the vote to raise women's status and, as the movement progressed, to improve their welfare, and if only to achieve these more limited aims they were prepared to assert women's difference from men. Increasingly, feminists insisted on the necessity of increasing state intervention in the domestic sphere and hence the need for women's participation *as* women in the state (Holton, 1986, p. 15).

There are many reasons why it took so long for women to get the vote, not the least of which has to do with party politics; the fear on the part of the Liberals and later the Labour Party that a vote for (middle-class) women would be a vote for the Tories, and the general hostility among Conservatives to such a radical measure (Rover, 1967, p. 181). But probably the most important was simply inertia: up until 1908 there was such indifference to womens' suffrage that there was not even an anti-suffrage organisation (Harrison, 1978, p. 17).

Nevertheless such arguments as there were against women's suffrage are interesting because they give us an indication of the extent to which the demand for the vote challenged the hegemonic cult of domesticity by reworking its elements in new ways. While some of these arguments were highly specific to the campaign itself – it was held, for example, that women did not need the vote because of the reforms that a male parliament had introduced on their behalf – most were more general and repeat the terms in which women were positioned in classical liberalism. First, it was held that there were natural differences between the sexes which suited women for the private domestic sphere (Harrison, 1978, pp. 60–70). This was elaborated into the argument that women's special influence as women would be lost were they to try to extend it to the public sphere. This was, for example, the focus of an influential letter published and signed by numerous prominent women (or as one feminist pointed out, wives of prominent men) (Hollis, 1979, p. 329), who argued that women's influence was effective only when they remained close to their 'natural position and functions' and relied on the guidance of 'the more highly trained and developed judgement of men' (quoted in Lewis, 1987, p. 411). Second, it was maintained that either women did not need the vote because husband and wife agreed, or, if they did not agree, women should not be granted the vote because it would 'introduce discord into every family' (quoted in Lewis, 1987, p. 254; Harrison, 1978, p. 70). And third, it was feared that women would indeed influence politics in a feminine way and this would not be for the common good; they might enforce unduly exigent moral standards (Banks, 1981, pp. 131–2) and they would indeed turn the state towards social welfare and towards partisan issues rather than the good of the whole (Hollis, 1979, pp. 305–6). All these arguments reiterate the most important features of women's position in classical liberalism: women are naturally subordinate in the private sphere and they *must* be subordinate there if there is to be unity and harmony in the home; and difference must be excluded from the public sphere in the interests of the common good. As we have seen, the use made by feminists of liberal-democratic principles challenged these fundamental assumptions of the classical liberal opposition between masculine public and feminine private spheres.

To sum up the counter-hegemonic project of first-wave feminism as it has been presented here, then, it has been argued that, using the undecidability of Victorian liberalism between women as self-determining individuals identical to men and women as having specific duties and functions in the private domestic sphere which made them different from men, as well as the explicit legitimation of difference in the public sphere that was the result of the articulation of liberalism and democracy, feminists contested the classical liberal opposition between public and private and contributed to its institution in new, more complex forms. To some extent these confounded the association of the feminine with the private domestic sphere and the masculine with the public sphere. The private domestic sphere retained its identity as the place of 'natural' love and care for particular others, but it was at the same time constructed as a place in which universal principles of freedom and equality, *opposed* to this love and care in classical liberalism, were to be applied, both in law and more widely in terms of informal personal relationships. At the same time the public sphere was reconfigured. First, in the new institutions of the workhouse, asylum, orphanage, and so on, a new area, difficult to place in terms of the older opposition between public and private, was carved out. This is sometimes referred to as 'the social'. Although not created by women, it had a specifically feminine inflection from the beginning. (See Donzelot, 1979, for a critical analysis of the invention of 'the social' in nineteenth- and early twentieth-century France and of women's influence on it.) And second, the difference between the sexes was brought into the public sphere as a valid topic for consideration in a democratic polity.

This last point is complicated because clearly sex was not the only, or even the most important difference claiming recognition in the public sphere: class differences in particular cut across and often overrode the differences between the sexes in the nineteenth century so that there was not always a simple difference between the sexes, but rather multiple differences arising from combinations of sex and class (Phillips, 1987a, ch. 4). Furthermore, the feminist assertion of sexual difference faltered once the vote was won and it was realised, in the words of Sylvia Pankhurst, that society would not be 'regenerated by enfranchised womanhood as by a magic wand' (quoted in Bouchier, 1983, p. 15). Although in the years immediately following the enfranchisement of women over 30 some legislation was passed (mainly concerning the reform of marriage, child custody and entry into the professions), very few women were elected, women never voted as a 'sex-class' and the unity of the feminist movement that had been sustained in the campaign for the vote was shattered (Bryson, 1992, pp. 98–100). The feminist movement was split in two over the question of how sexual difference should be represented in politics, a split that was in some measure due to different ways of articulating class and sex. Equal rights feminists held that difference should only be represented in order to press for gender-neutral laws and institutions; although they had no theory of androgyny they saw assertions of difference as problematic for women's equality. For 'new feminists', on the other hand, the validation of sexual difference was seen as an end in itself and as a means to 'real' equality between the sexes. It was this 'new feminist' perspective that contributed most to yet another version of liberalism, that of the liberal-democratic welfare state.

5 Post-war Liberal-Democracy and the Undecidability of Women

Liberalism in twentieth-century Britain has been split between 'new liberalism', which enjoyed pre-eminence in the first half, and neo-liberalism, which has become increasingly important in the last 20 years, without, however, being able to displace the former completely. Although very different in many ways, they are similar insofar as both depend on the constitutive undecidability of women between the private domestic sphere and the public sphere of state/civil society. In this respect they are also similar to classical liberalism. In practice, a Millian version of liberalism, which positions women as individuals *within* the private domestic sphere, has also been influential. In the final decade of the twentieth century, it will be argued, women are positioned as undecidable in three different versions of liberalism, each of which has contributed to the social and political practices in which actual women are engaged.

What is the relation between feminism and this composite of liberalisms? Liberalism no longer provides the guiding ideology of feminism as it did in the nineteenth century; in Britain that place has been taken by socialism, altered under the influence of radical feminism to take women's issues into account. But because of the historical importance of liberalism, transformed as we have seen in the nineteenth and early twentieth century into liberal-democracy, it is nevertheless the case that the relationship between liberalism and feminism remains central to any understanding of feminism's impact and potential.

The form of this chapter is somewhat different from that of the previous two because the most important feminist work on liberalism in the twentieth century has been the critique of institutions, and of the liberal principles embedded in them, rather than of political philosophy *per se*.[1] This is the case for the most significant development of twentieth-century liberal-democracy, the welfare state, which has been subject to extensive feminist criticism, as well as the legislation introduced to deal with gender inequalities which has been widely criticised as inadequate. We shall begin the analysis with a brief history of

103

the ideas of welfare liberalism, with particular reference to its relation to older versions of liberalism. We shall then examine the feminist critique of the patriarchal welfare state, again focussing on the work of Carole Pateman. A deconstruction of the Beveridge Report will follow; although this is obviously not a work of political philosophy on a level with Locke's or Mill's work, it was influenced by New Liberalism, and is a crucial text insofar as it was introduced virtually intact as the National Insurance element of the welfare state. We will then go on to look at the relation between second-wave feminism and some of the most important liberal institutions of the second half of the twentieth century including, in the final section, the Thatcherite project of neo-liberalism.

WELFARE LIBERALISM AND THE UNDECIDABILITY OF WOMEN

Welfare Liberalism

New liberalism was an innovative and dynamic rethinking of the precepts of the liberal tradition which aimed to have a significant impact on politics in the late nineteenth and early twentieth centuries. Imbued with a strong sense of public service and strengthened by the conviction that they could provide industrial society with the new political direction it needed, new liberals actively sought to influence political parties, movements and processes. The extent to which they succeeded is, however, somewhat controversial.

For Michael Freeden, an historian of ideas who has worked in detail on new liberal philosophy and its impact, even if the influence of ideas on political practices is difficult to assess, it is clear that the new liberals are responsible for setting a framework within which social welfare was made acceptable to those of broadly liberal persuasion and which enabled the later development of ideas on the welfare state. As Freeden sees it, the new liberals reconciled social welfare and individual freedom in a way which justified extensive state intervention in liberal terms, even if later legislators and administrators were not fully conscious of the principles they were upholding (Freeden, 1990; Freeden, 1978, pp. 247–9). Martin Bentley, on the other hand, takes the view that since there is no evidence of new liberal influence within any of the political parties after the demise of the Liberal Party in 1916 (where anyway it was only briefly significant), nor of progressive liberal motivation on the part of individuals within those parties, new liberal ideas must be held to have had minimal political impact on the setting up of the welfare state in 1945 (Bentley, 1987, ch. 8).

One problem with Bentley's argument is that, as Addison has argued, although it was the Labour Party that was the most effective in pressing for social reform, the ideas which informed the welfare state were largely developed outside political parties altogether, by non-party reformers and professionals (Addison, 1994, p. 40). This is true, for example, of the Beveridge Report with which we are concerned here. Although Beveridge was of liberal sympathies all his life, with some connections to new liberalism through his Oxford college and through Toynbee Hall where he worked as a youth, he did not join the party until after the Second World War, seeing himself primarily as a civil servant (Harris, 1977). Beveridge was not a new liberal, and he was in some respects at odds with new liberal thought, but, as we shall see, the version of welfare liberalism he developed and which was put into practice as the social insurance element of the welfare state, was informed by certain of their theoretical assumptions and conclusions.

New liberalism has both continuities and discontinuities with the older versions of liberalism we have looked at in previous chapters. The new liberals themselves saw it as an advance on older versions in the sense that it was adapted to a new social and political reality while at the same time it offered an understanding which would allow the further progress of society to be achieved. To this end new liberals were actively engaged in the attempt to persuade influential members of the ruling liberal establishment, the general public and, to some extent, the nascent Labour Party, of the importance of their way of thinking, through journalism, study groups, public lectures and so on. Here we shall limit our considerations to the work of three thinkers, R.G. Ritchie, L.T. Hobhouse and J.A. Hobson, the most theoretically rigorous of those involved in the counter-hegemonic project of new liberalism.[2] The most important aspect of their thought was the re-evaluation of the relation between the state and the individual; their concern with individual rights clearly links them to the liberal tradition, but their rethinking of this relation seems, in some ways, to represent quite a new departure in liberal political philosophy.

New liberals reinterpreted the liberal emphasis on individual freedom as primarily a matter of rational restraint. They argued that old liberals, like Locke, were concerned above all to end *arbitrary* restraint with the rule of law, and that to think of freedom as the ending of restraint in general was incoherent since it could only mean the 'tyranny of the strongest' (Ritchie, 1891, pp. 83–5; Hobhouse, 1994, pp. 10–11). As Ritchie pointed out, developing Mill's ideas on the similarities and differences between the constraints of society and of the state, state interference is sometimes necessary to protect individuals' freedom from the arbitrary power of social opinion or of other individuals in society (Ritchie, 1891, pp. 91–4). In this respect, new liberalism can be seen as drawing the logical conclusions of the liberal tradition more rigorously, or as emphasising aspects of liberalism which were under-appreciated by old liberals.

On the other hand, however, new liberals were inclined also to argue that liberalism had to adapt to the new conditions of industrial society in order to ensure its essential principles, the maximisation of individual liberty and equality. To this end, they argued that liberals should support the closer regulation of contracts between employers and employees (in factory legislation, for example, and through the exertion of trade union power) in order to ensure the genuine equality of the contracting parties and therefore genuine freedom of consent. While nineteenth-century liberals, they argued, had never been unequivocally in favour of *laissez-faire* economic principles – Cobden, for example, arguing against the monopoly of land for just these reasons – the increasing collectivisation and growing inequalities of industrial society meant a greater degree of state intervention was now necessary to regulate contracts which could no longer be seen simply as individual arrangements (Hobhouse, 1994, pp. 37–48; Ritchie, 1891, pp. 120–1; Hobson, 1909, pp. 3–4). Similarly, they advocated a greater realisation of equality of individual opportunities, with particular reference to the controversial question of the state provision of education (Hobhouse, 1994, p. 15; Hobson, 1909, pp. 93–4; Ritchie, 1891, pp. 116–17). Finally, in Hobhouse's view at least, the state had been democratised with the extension of the franchise and professionalised with the reform of the civil service and, less governed by the interests of the ruling class, could be a more positive force for social progress than earlier liberals had feared (Hobhouse, 1994, pp. 123–35).

The main theoretical innovation of what Hobhouse called 'reconstructive' liberalism, as opposed to the earlier liberalism which was 'destructive' of authoritarianism, was the new liberal view of the individual as inseparable from society. According to this theory, which Hobhouse rightly described as the element of new liberal thinking which was furthest from old liberal thought (Hobhouse, 1994, p. 64), genuine individual liberty requires self-realisation, which can only be achieved through social development. The new liberal theory of individual freedom

builds on T.H. Green's idea of 'positive liberty', though Green himself did not draw the collectivist conclusions later liberals were to elaborate on the basis of his philosophy (Weiler, 1982, pp. 38–40). According
to his idea of freedom, popularised by Ritchie and further elaborated
by Hobhouse, freedom does not consist in freedom to do as one pleases,
which is mere licence, but in 'the scope given to the individual for
exercising all his capacities of self-development' (Ritchie, 1891, p. 144).
For new liberals, individual capacities are those of humans as rational,
and at the same time essentially social, beings. Given the complex
division of labour of modern societies, an individual could not even
survive physically without others; but further, it is through socialisation
that each individual becomes themselves (Hobhouse, 1994, p. 60). It
is social conditions, then, which make it possible for the individual to
realise its innate capacity for rational self-control and the self-determination of its own personality (the use of the term 'it' is Hobhouse's,
though he generally uses 'he' [Hobhouse, 1994, p. 53]).

It is from this view of the individual as essentially social that Hobhouse
derives his theory of rights. Given the presupposition that every individual is equally important and that rights are therefore to be accorded
impartially, he argues that individual rights can only be grounded in
the common good; that is, in the good which allows for the self-realisation
of each and every individual (Hobhouse, 1994, pp. 60–5). For Hobhouse,
as for Green, 'the individual finds his own good in the common good'
(p. 61). He explicitly contrasts this with the views of old liberals for
whom individual rights were prior to the formation of the state, arguing that on this conception it becomes virtually impossible to imagine
how the conflict between individual interests and common welfare can
be resolved (Hobhouse, 1904, pp. 131–7). Hobhouse sees Mill as spanning
the old and new liberalism since Mill assumes, as we have seen, the
ultimate compatibility of social and individual well-being. Hobhouse
sees this as the most important point of Mill's theory of representative
democracy: the vote is a means of binding the individual and society
in mutual responsibility (Hobhouse, 1994, pp. 53–4). Like Mill, Hobhouse and other new liberals assumed a teleological progress of history
towards harmony.

The view of society from which new liberal ideas of the intrinsic
relation between society and the individual are derived is the analogy
of society as an organism, a truism for social thinkers of the late nineteenth and early twentieth centuries (even if they disagreed on how
the metaphor should be interpreted). Society is not, as Locke would
have it, an aggregate of individuals; it is a complex set of interrelated

institutions, governed by social and economic laws of development and potentially susceptible to direction by a rational, enlightened state. And by the extension of this analogy using evolutionary theory, new liberals were able to adopt what in retrospect seems a naively optimistic view of the possibility of realising a society in which there was a harmony between the principles of common good instituted by the rationalised, democratic state and the development of the personality of each self-disciplining, self-determining individual within that society (Hobhouse, 1968; Hobson, 1909, ch. IV).[3]

Their theory of the individual and society as inseparable also led new liberals to rethink individual rights to private property. They saw private wealth itself as essentially social since it is created using a system of production and distribution which draws on 'the whole available means of civilisation', and guaranteed only by the organised force of society in the state. Wealth is, then, to be used for the benefit of all and private property rights are only to be upheld where this is functional for the economy (Hobhouse, 1994, pp. 91–101). Hobson goes so far as to advocate what he describes as the communist slogan 'from each according to his ability, to each according to his needs' as the ethical ideal towards which every civilised community should be committed as a principle of progress (Hobson, 1976, p. 139). For him state intervention in the economy is necessary since otherwise its manifest irrationality make injustice inevitable and progress impossible (Hobson, 1976, pp. 131 and 189–212).

However, in spite of their views on private property and the importance of the state as the expression of the common good, and despite what the new liberals themselves saw as tendencies towards socialism in their thought, they frequently reiterated their adherence to the liberal tradition. It is in opposition to socialism that new liberals tend to emphasise the importance of the public/private distinction as a central tenet of liberal thought, though they use the terms less frequently than older liberals and with less assurance. Ritchie, for example, is in agreement with Mill that there should be a private sphere of non-interference in individual freedom, but he argues strongly that since man is a social being and there are, therefore, no purely self-regarding actions, there is no *a priori* principle which can delimit that sphere in advance of any particular instance in which it is in question. According to Ritchie, and paradoxically from the point of view of older liberalism, the sphere of individual privacy is 'an ideal, differing at different times, always more or less vague, and to be permanently secured only by the help of a strong, and vigorous, and enlightened State' (Ritchie, 1891, p. 99).

Hobhouse and Hobson are especially concerned to differentiate their theories from socialism by insisting that there will always be a place for private enterprise in a liberal political economy. Hobson argues that state-planning of the economy is only possible with respect to standard physiological needs, and that since individuals will always have different tastes and interests, there will always be scope for private initiative in meeting these individual preferences (Hobson, 1976, p. 174). Hobhouse is prepared to adopt the title 'liberal socialism' for his theory, but on condition that it is distinguished from other versions of socialism which he takes to be anti-democratic, dismissive of individual freedom and undermining of voluntary self-help and mutual aid (Hobhouse, 1994, pp. 81–6). Although he rarely uses the term 'private', these distinctions are clearly intended to delimit a sphere which should be outside state regulation.

New liberals do not, however, see the domestic sphere as private in this way. This is evident in the use they make of the example of women's rights to protection from the tyranny of husbands to illustrate the extension of state intervention which guarantees rather than undermines individual freedom (Ritchie, 1891, p. 92). In fact, Hobhouse includes these rights in a separate section, headed 'Domestic Liberty', of his analysis of progressive liberal legislation (Hobhouse, 1994, pp. 18–19). Following Mill, then, the new liberals distinguish between privacy as the rights of individuals to non-interference and the space of the domestic sphere as a private realm. This distinction becomes less clear in the social insurance programme which was influenced by new liberalism and instituted in Beveridge's plan for the welfare state.

One reason why it is difficult to assess the influence of new liberalism on Beveridge's thought is the fact that he rarely discussed the principles underlying his plans for the welfare state in theoretical terms. He preferred to justify his views in the pragmatic terms of national efficiency rather than those of moral and political philosophy. However, as Jose Harris has pointed out, despite his predilection for empirical research and practical solutions to social problems, the plans he proposed for social reform made remarkably little use of research findings and on one occasion he explicitly stated that ultimately the merits and demerits of planning would have to be judged on political criteria, with reference not to economic efficiency but to the problem of the constitution and powers of the supreme authority in the State' (Harris, 1977, p. 473 and Beveridge, quoted p. 328). It is not too far-fetched, then, to see issues of liberal principle as underlying his proposals. This is not to say, however, that Beveridge was simply a descendent of the new liberals with whom he associated in his youth. As Harris has also pointed out, he was a highly eclectic thinker who in the course of his career adopted virtually every point of view available to liberals of his time, even going beyond liberalism to adopt views on economics which were more in sympathy with the socialism of the Fabian Webbs than with Keynsian liberals immediately after the Second World War (p. 2). Beveridge did, however, retain certain guiding theoretical presuppositions from new liberalism throughout his career.

Probably the most important of these was his underlying commitment to social holism. This has much in common with the new liberal view that society is an organism which should be directed by a rational state, and that it is possible to reconcile the rights and duties of citizens guaranteed by such a state with individual freedom (Harris, 1977, p. 472). In Beveridge's view there should be an organic relationship between the state, voluntary organisations and private individuals to ensure individual freedom and social solidarity. His concern with individual freedom was primarily with freedom from what he called the Five Giants, 'the social evils of Want, Disease, Ignorance, Squalor and Idleness' (Beveridge, 1986, p. 231). This idea of freedom is very similar to that of the new liberals; although Beveridge put more emphasis on its negative aspect, the *freedom from* arbitrary restraint, it is also positive in that it involves the *freedom* to develop human and individual capacities. Furthermore Beveridge comes close to new liberal thinking insofar as he also maintained a commitment to what he called 'essential freedoms', to a private sphere of non-interference in individual actions. For Beveridge, as for the new liberals, individual freedom is contingent on a type of social development which should provide the conditions of possibility for the realisation of human capacities without interfering unduly with what should remain private concerns. Social progress is only possible along these lines, he held, when there is social solidarity: when every member of society is committed to the freedom of all (Harris, 1977, p. 418). According to Beveridge, harmony between social and individual ends should be the goal, and paradoxically it seems, also the means of social progress (compare Ritchie, 1891, pp. 102–4).

In his belief in progress towards the reconciliation of individual freedom and the common good, Beveridge also shared an evolutionary frame of reference with the new liberals. He seems to have been much more cautious, however, in his belief in the possibility of the realisation of social harmony. He lacked the quasi-metaphysical convictions of the new liberals, though he does seem to have supposed that individuals would behave in a moral, rather than a self-interested way, once the social and political conditions he advocated were instituted. (For example, he anticipated that the new power workers would gain through policies of full employment and organised trade unions would not lead them to act solely in their own interests; he did not, therefore, expect inflation to be a problem for post-war economic policy [Harris, 1977, p. 437].) Insofar as Beveridge explicitly theorised his views on social evolution he seems, however, to have been closer to Social Darwinism than to new liberalism. For Beveridge there was a congruence between the nation and the race and he was particularly concerned with the problem raised by eugenicists at that time, that the practice of birth control by more reponsible sectors of society would lead to the deterioration of the national stock' within Britain and in relation to other, non-white nations (Harris, 1977, p. 341). It is in part because of such fears that Beveridge enthusiastically took up Eleanor Rathbone's proposals for Family Allowances.

Apart from their most profound assumptions concerning the possibility of harmony between state planning and individual freedom, probably the most significant common ground beween Beveridge and the new liberals is their economic theories; they were all attempting to find a middle way between free-market liberalism and communism. As we have seen, Hobson, the foremost new liberal economic theorist, retained a place for private enterprise whilst emphasising the necessity of state planning in order to mitigate the injustices of the free market. Similarly, Beveridge came very close to socialism – his ideas were indistinguishable from those of social democrats immediately after the Second World War according to Harris – but he retained a belief in the most important principle of liberalism, that there should be a private sphere of individual freedom opposed to the power of the state.

Beveridge gave a large part to the state in managing the economy, to the extent of agreeing with the socialist Webbs rather than the liberal Keynes for a brief period, that full employment would be better achieved by the state directly providing work rather than by regulating the demand for workers through the stimulation of consumption (Harris, 1977, pp. 428–30). But ultimately he situated himself in the liberal tradition. He argued that, unlike socialists, liberals were not prepared to sacrifice 'essential liberties' for the sake of state control or sectional interests (Beveridge, 1986, pp. 228–9). The liberties Beveridge saw as essential are the freedoms of classical liberalism, those which define the private sphere and guarantee the rights of the individual against the state:

the intimate personal liberties (worship, speech, writing, study, teaching; spending of personal income; choice of occupation) and on the other hand, the political liberties (assembly and associations for industrial and political purposes) which are necessary to prevent the establishing of arbitrary power.

(Beveridge, 1986, p. 231)

So, although the power of the state should be used wherever necessary to protect citizens against 'the Five Giants', and although, according to Beveridge this justifies interference with some uses of private property (such as the right to set up industries without planning permission), for Beveridge, since the aim of a liberal welfare state is equality of freedom, and not equality *per se*, the power of the state must be kept within determinate limits and the negative freedom of individuals assured (Beveridge, 1986).

The welfare state instituted after the Second World War in Britain may, then, be seen as the institution of a form of liberalism in which the classical liberal opposition between public and private remains but in which state intervention is extended far beyond the limits set for it by old liberals. This is the case in the Keynesian economic policies, which Beveridge came to accept and which provided the basis of government until the 1970s, in which state planning was extended into what was previously considered to be the private sphere of production and distribution. And in Beveridgean social insurance, policies are enacted which regularise an extension of the public into what was previously considered the private domestic sphere. As we shall see, there is some overlap between the private sphere of negative liberty to which the Beveridgean welfare state is committed and the private sphere which is the domestic realm, but the two are certainly not synonymous as they were for Locke; the household became a major object of social and economic policies with the institution of the liberal welfare state in 1945.

Although we have discussed Beveridge as an individual who was influenced by new liberal thinking, and this is justified to the extent that he was highly autocratic and highly influential on the form of social insurance that was introduced in 1945, the welfare state should not, however, be seen as solely liberal, not even as solely new liberal; it must also be seen as democratic in the Lefortian sense. It should be seen as the extension of democratic rights to new areas of society as a result of pressure from social movements, rather than simply as the result of theoretical innovation within the liberal tradition. Beveridge interpreted and codified a widespread agreement on what should be the ideal relation between citizens and the state and as a result was made a popular hero in 1942 when his Report was published (Harris, 1977, pp. 426–8). The popular acclaim which greeted the Report was probably in part a product of the media orchestration of the event and in part a product of the sense of national solidarity promoted during wartime, but it is also reasonable to suppose that the pressure which had been growing from the Labour Party, sections of the Liberal Party, women's groups and trades unions since the late nineteenth century for a greater degree of state intervention to equalize social conditions also had their effect (Pugh, 1993, pp. 78–81; Rowbotham, 1986). To the extent that the demands from such groups were made to the state (initially local councils were more important than national government) they were linked to the extension of the franchise and in this way to liberal-democracy narrowly conceived, but insofar as they go beyond rights simply to participate in the election of government, they represent the extension of democracy into new areas. In this respect the welfare state should be seen as liberal-democratic, not in the sense of liberal democracy which makes provision for certain procedures for the election of government, but in the sense that it institutes Lefortian democratic rights within a liberal framework.

The question of the impact of feminism as a social movement on this new democratised liberal political formation is currently a matter of some controversy among feminist historians. The feminism which was dominant in the first half of the twentieth century was, interestingly, closer to the new liberalism than to the old, although there is little historical material from which to investigate the connection (Alberti, 1996, pp. 17–18 and 32). Although there were feminist groups who maintained that equality required identical treatment for men and women, women's groups tended to argue from a 'new feminist' or maternalist perspective that in order for women to achieve 'real equality', their specific capacities and responsibilities as mothers should be recognised (Bacchi, 1990, pp. 51–8). Because of their affiliation with the ascendent labour movement, these groups were more powerful than those more closely allied to what is conventionally thought of as the liberal position, the view that any recognition of men and women as different is more likely to contribute to inequality than to ameliorate it (Dale and Foster, 1986, ch. 1; Pugh, 1992, pp. 236–44).

Jane Lewis argues that feminism had little influence on the formation of the welfare state. She maintains that although women were highly active in local politics and welfare work in the late nineteenth and early twentieth centuries, and although they were sometimes in-spired by maternalism, they were at least, if not more, as concerned with the generally acknowledged 'social problem' of poverty as with the equality of the sexes. Party political allegiance motivated these women as much as solidarity with other women so that the issue of women's and children's welfare was seen more as a matter for the labour movement than for feminists. Moreover, once welfare became a matter of 'high politics' after 1916 women were no longer able to exercise any influence over its development (Lewis, 1994).

Certainly, it is the case that maternalists were not necessarily moti-vated by feminism – Mrs Ward, for example, who (in)famously cam-paigned against women's suffrage, was a maternalist. And the issue is very much complicated by the fact that maternalist proposals could be endorsed by politicians who were unsympathetic to feminism of any description, aimed as they were at supporting and validating women as wives and mothers (Pugh, 1993, p. 115). Furthermore, it is gener-ally agreed that women's contributions to welfare institutions were marginalised with the bureaucratisation of the centralised welfare state (Koven, 1993). However, it would seem that Lewis has somewhat overstated her case.

First, as Pat Thane has argued, although the role of elite adminis-trators was more important than that of political parties in the setting up the welfare state, local government, voluntary organisations and political parties were also influential and women played an active role in all of these, succeeding to a limited extent in shaping policy pro-posals through their social investigations and campaigning activities (Thane, 1993). Secondly, the influence of women like Eleanor Rathbone, who had close personal connections to the ruling establishment as well as being the leader of the National Union of Societies for Equal Citi-zenship in the 1920s and Independent MP in the 1930s and 1940s, must be taken into account. Although family allowances were not awarded to women to reward their unpaid care as Rathbone initially envisaged along 'new feminist' lines, but rather for pro-natalist reasons and to keep wages down, she was influential in ensuring that they were paid to women rather than men when they were finally instituted in 1945 (Lewis, 1991; Stocks, 1949; Beveridge, 1949).

Feminists seem to have had mixed reactions to Beveridge's pro-posals. Some, in particular 'new feminists' like Rathbone and Vera Brittan, were enthusiastic about the welfare state. Brittan saw it as having transformed the 'women's question':

The welfare state has been both cause and consequence of the second great change by which women have moved ... from rivalry with
men to a new recognition of their unique value as women.

(quoted in Dale and Foster, 1986, p. 3)

From the older liberal feminist perspective, predictably, it was argued
that women should have been accorded identical rights with men. And
still others were critical from what seems to have been a maternalist
perspective, arguing that Beveridge's proposals had not gone far enough
towards ensuring women's welfare and that in addition to family allowances, married women should have been paid an allowance as a
wage for their job (Harris, 1977, p. 403).

Beveridge was concerned in his Report to recognise the specificity
of women's capacities and tasks and to ensure that their rights and
duties as citizens were defined accordingly. According to his view,
women should stand in a different relation to the state from men since
they have different social and biological duties, and justice requires
that the state recognise their position as wives and mothers in the domestic
sphere, a position which is different from but equal to that of men in
the labour-market. Second-wave feminists have dealt harshly with
Beveridge's proposals in this respect, much more harshly than most
feminists of the time, criticising them as contributing to women's dependence on men and to their status as second-class citizens.

Pateman's Analysis of the Patriarchal Welfare State

As a critic of liberalism who is sensitive to the actual construction of
social and political institutions along liberal lines, the most interesting
analysis of the welfare state is that of Carole Pateman.[4] In 'The Patriarchal Welfare State' Pateman again puts the opposition between feminine
private and masculine public spheres at the centre of her analysis, arguing that the welfare state institutes a two-tier system of citizenship
premised on this opposition (Pateman, 1989a, p. 183). According to
Pateman, only men are full citizens of the welfare state, principally
because they are seen as 'independent' breadwinners, while women are
second-class citizens because, as we have seen, they have been historically constructed as dependants.[5] The welfare state pays relatively
high benefits to those who have contributed to it financially, through
insurance from their earnings, while it pays more meagre benefits to
'dependants' or 'private' persons who may have made little or no direct
financial contribution and who tend, therefore, to be seen as undeserving

'scroungers' (pp. 187–8). This two-tier system, according to Pateman, is a product of, and a contribution to, the opposition between masculine public and feminine private spheres: men are independent individuals in the public sphere of paid employment and are first-class citizens by right of this position while women are dependent wives and mothers in the private domestic sphere of unpaid care and, contributing to the welfare state indirectly, through this care, have an inferior citizenship. As Pateman puts it:

> Women are not incorporated as citizens like men, but as members of the family, a sphere separate from (or in social exile from) civil society and the state. The family is essential to civil society and the state but it is constituted on a different basis from the rest of conventional social life, having its own ascriptive principles of association . . . constituted by love, ties of blood, natural subjection and particularity, and in which [women] are governed by men. The public world of universal citizenship is an association of free and equal individuals, a sphere of property, rights and contract – and of men who interact as formally equal citizens.
>
> (pp. 182–3)

At the same time Pateman again recognises the 'paradoxes and contradictions' of women's citizenship in the welfare state (p. 185). First, she argues that 'welfare policies have reached across from public to private and helped uphold a patriarchal structure of familial life' (p. 183). In other words, in the welfare state the private sphere becomes the object of detailed legislation such that it is quite a different from the private domestic sphere of classical liberalism; it is a form of private life constructed and sustained by an interventionist state. Despite this difference, however, Pateman describes both the private sphere of welfare state liberalism and that of classical liberalism in the same terms: as constituted by love, care and subordination, in opposition to the public sphere of universal rights and contract. And second, in practice, Pateman notes that the welfare state has actually helped *undermine* the traditional family as women have been enabled to become directly dependent on the state, rather than indirectly as men's dependants (p. 196). Despite her assertion that the welfare state maintains patriarchy, then, Pateman also recognises the paradox that it challenges it too, offering a 'basis for women's autonomous citizenship' in the independent provision it makes for women and children (p. 185). She maintains, however, that women cannot be full citizens on this basis since under current arrangements citizenship is tied to employment. Women can only be full citizens insofar as they can be like men, and insofar as they are women they can only ever be 'lesser men' (p. 197).

A deconstruction of the Beveridge Report, which provided the blueprint for the National Insurance scheme that was one of the pillars of the welfare state and which has since only been modified, not substantially altered, will show, on my account, that Pateman does not give sufficient weight to these 'paradoxes and contradictions' (though she does not completely erase them as she did from the readings of liberalism we have examined in previous chapters). While it is undoubtedly the case that women *as* women, that is as wives or mothers in the private sphere, are citizens in a different, and in some respects (in the value of benefits they receive, for example) inferior sense, a deconstruction of the Beveridge Report will show the undecidability of women between two forms of citizenship in relation to the public/private opposition which do not exactly map onto Pateman's independent/dependant dichotomy. It is important to separate out different identities of women in relation to the welfare state: women as workers and as mothers both have a direct relation to the state, while as wives their relation to it is mediated through their husbands. It is this latter status that puts women outside full citizenship. It is not women *as* women who are outside full citizenship; rather women are undecidably placed as both inside and outside it and it is from this undecidability that their inferior status follows. It is important to separate out these different aspects of women's citizenship precisely because the liberal-democratic welfare state is innovative in relation to other forms of liberalism; it involves the recognition of democratic rights for women that are tied to their specific difference from men as unpaid carers in the private sphere. If feminism has not been very successful in extending the democratic rights of women *as* women this is not, as the feminist critics of liberalism as essentially masculine suggest, because of the inherent logic of liberalism as exclusionary of that difference. In practice, liberal-democracy has instituted women's citizenship in the welfare state, at least in part, *on the basis* of women's specificity.

The Beveridge Report

It is much more difficult to deconstruct Beveridge's text along Derridean lines than either Mill's or Locke's because he is concerned with gradations rather than absolutes, with the ordering of empirical facts rather than the metaphysical foundations of political philosophy. But insofar as he does posit a binary opposition between public and private (though he does not often use the terms himself) it is possible to see how 'women' works as an undecidable which is simultaneously the condition of possibility and impossibility of this opposition.[6] Women are undecidable insofar as they have a direct relation to the state as individuals who *must* be insured but, at the same time, as married women they are also positioned outside a direct relation to the state in the private sphere in which security in the face of the contingencies of life is a matter of personal responsibility for 'the individual and his family' (Beveridge, 1966, p. 7). Women stand both inside the public sphere of state compulsion and outside it, in the private domestic sphere of spontaneous co-operation and private initiative in which man and wife are described as a 'team' (p. 49).[7] But because married women have, at one and the same time, a direct relationship with the state and an indirect one, there is a constant interplay of undecidability between women's position in the public and the private such that ultimately the opposition between compulsion and freedom is unsustainable. It is not, however, the unsustainability of this opposition that concerns us here (in contrast to previous chapters) and arguably, since Beveridge did not see himself as engaged in philosophy, it would not have worried him either; what is important are the terms of the undecidability itself and the way in which it has contributed to women's ambiguous citizenship status.

It is one of the principal aims of the Beveridge Report to differentiate between citizens in order to treat like cases alike and different cases as different. As Beveridge puts it:

> the general principle underlying the Plan for Social Security [is that] of unification of responsibility in order to avoid needless and harmful differences, combined with classification, that is to say, with giving to each need the treatment most appropriate for that need.
>
> (Beveridge, 1966, p. 45)

Beveridge's scheme is universalist but not in the sense of classical liberalism: justice is substantive and involves the recognition of concrete social circumstances and not just formal civil and political rights. To this end he develops a detailed classification of citizens based on their employment status, age, state of health and, in the case of women, their status as wives and mothers. Housewives are a distinct class of persons, with benefits adjusted, according to Beveridge, to their special needs. Within this class there are, however, several different ways of being a housewife and they each have rather a different relation to the state. We should note, though, that there is another class of women in Beveridge's scheme, single women: they are treated as identical to single men insofar as they pay the same rate of insurance and receive the same sickness and unemployment benefits (pp. 9–11). The first group of married women are similar to these single women in that they pay the same amount of insurance, but they are different because married women may choose to make no financial contribution to National Insurance at all and if they do decide to contribute as individuals they receive reduced rates of benefits (pp. 50–1).[8] With this group we move out of a straightforward relation of compulsion between the individual and the state and into a more indeterminate area, part compulsion, part freedom. It is indeterminate, not simply because the housewife herself is presented with a choice rather than being compelled to insure herself, but because the justification for the reduction of benefits is that a wife's rent will be paid out of a husband's earnings so she needs less to live on (p. 50). Clearly this depends on the informal distribution of resources in the home and so on private relations, private both in the sense of voluntary and in the sense of domestic. Here then, although married women may contribute financially to the state and receive benefits directly from it, their relation to it is partially mediated through that of their husbands. It is not only different from that of other citizens in the sense of involving different rights and duties, it is also different insofar as married women do not relate directly to the state as individuals, but indirectly as 'quasi-individuals', members of 'teams' headed by individuals who are male. The second group of married women who work are those who choose not to pay contributions. They are in the same relation to the state as the third group, who do not work outside the home and do not pay insurance contributions to the state, that is a relation which is virtually eclipsed by that of their husbands. It is husbands who make insurance contributions and wives have no rights to sickness and unemployment benefits, nor to pensions except through their husbands' contributions (pp. 50–1). These women are almost entirely outside a direct relation to the state as individuals, and almost entirely in the private sphere of voluntary arrangements. Not quite, however, since, as citizens who are part of the totality of the social security scheme, they also have a direct relation to the state. And it is this undecidability of women which makes the private domestic sphere possible: without the difference Beveridge makes between husbands and wives there would be no private domestic sphere for insurance purposes, since all would stand in the same relation of compulsion to the state.[9] And at the same time it makes it impossible as a rigorously delimited, self-present category: as part of the social security system everyone *must* be in a direct relation to the state, and if women are situated in the private domestic sphere then compulsion must extend there too. The direct relation of a married woman to the state was to be represented by the marriage grant which she was to receive to mark the transition to her new status, her new rights and duties as a wife (p. 50). Beveridge saw this as optional, however, and it was never instituted. The direct relation remained in the insurance which husbands were compelled to make for wives, on pain of imprisonment (p. 142), against their own sickness, unemployment and old age and also against the peculiar risks of married women's 'occupation', divorce and widowhood (p. 134). (Beveridge drew an analogy between desertion by one's husband and an industrial accident [Harris, 1977, p. 406].) The state was to ensure that married women were protected if informal arrangements failed in the private sphere, but so long as they were actually married, women's direct relation to the state was mediated through their husbands and they were firmly positioned in the informal private sphere.

The position of women as mothers was, I would argue, somewhat different in this respect from that of women as wives: mothers retained their direct relation to the state, even in marriage. First, their relation was direct insofar as the state recognised their contribution to the nation *as* mothers. This is a theme which is constantly repeated throughout the Beveridge Report:

> In the next thirty years, housewives as mothers will have vital work to do in ensuring the adequate continuance of the British race and of British ideals in the world.
>
> (Beveridge, 1966, p. 53)

The term 'race' here gives us pause to ask exactly who is included here as contributing to the nation-state. Though black British women are technically included as citizens, in actual fact their motherhood has often been deemed inferior and has been subject to control through restrictive immigration and reproductive policies (Williams, 1991, pp. 315–16). To be more precise, then, the state recognised the contribution of *white* mothers, and some black mothers insofar as they were considered eligible, in benefits that were not always conditional on insurance contributions, as were those of men, single women and wives. Maternity grants and benefit (at a higher rate than sickness or unemployment benefit and intended to balance the lower rates of these benefits received by married women) to be granted for a statutory 13 weeks were dependent on insurance contributions, either of husbands, of working wives or, in the case of the 'small class' of unmarried mothers, of single women (Beveridge, 1966, pp. 50–1). But children's allowances were conditional only on women giving birth and caring for a child (or rather, for more than one child since the first-born received no allowance) and as such they were a recognition of mothers' direct contribution to the nation-state. Furthermore, the relation between women as mothers and the state is also direct insofar as family allowances were paid to women and not to their husbands. Although Beveridge constructed children's allowances as a safeguard against the poverty of families with children, rather than as the wages for mothers for which they were initially designed by Eleanor Rathbone, and although he did not specify to whom they were to be paid, when the Report was instituted feminist pressure ensured that they were paid directly to women as the member of the household responsible for children's welfare (Lewis, 1991, p. 87).

I submit, then, that the case made by Pateman, that women are not full citizens of the welfare state because their contributions are made by unpaid care in the private sphere rather than through paid work in the public sphere, can be refined by seeing women's citizenship as undecidable. It is undecidable insofar as women have both a direct and an indirect relation to the state; and it is in terms of the indirect relation that their citizenship status is inferior. It is not the case, as Pateman maintains, that women only achieve full citizenship insofar as they are like men. Women are like men in only one of the ways in which they are constructed in the Beveridge Report as individuals in direct relation to the state, that is, as single women. They also have full citizenship in their specific difference from men, as mothers. It is not women's difference from men *per se* that makes their citizenship status inferior, but their position as wives. In the Beveridge Report the state safeguards wives against insecurity only through husbands and it is insofar as mothers and wives are conflated that the citizenship status of women as different is inferior. The welfare state barely concerns itself with the private domestic arrangements between husband and wife and in this respect it neglects the wife's access to resources in the home, it neglects her welfare. And insofar as mothers are assumed, for the most part to be wives, beyond the specific provisions it makes for maternity it also neglects the welfare of women as mothers. It positively celebrates motherhood (even, if tentatively, that of the unmarried mother), as insured wives it allows women allowances to bring up children without needing to undertake paid work outside the home if they are widowed or separated (Beveridge, 1966, pp. 133–4) (though the latter were not implemented in practice [Johnson, 1990, p. 36]), but for the most part it assumes that husbands will provide for wives, both in the cases which the Report is designed to cover – sickness, unemployment, etc. – and in times of normal employment. Those women who do not have this provision 'fall through the meshes of insurance' and into the stigmatised, means-tested National Assistance scheme in which benefits are granted according to need rather than solely by right (p. 12). It is in this respect that the citizenship status of women as mothers is inferior, as women who are mothers but not wives. Pateman's analysis is correct, then, insofar as it is women's position as dependants that results in inferior citizenship status, but this should not be confused with women's difference from men, with the recognition of their specific capacities and responsibilities. As I have argued, women as mothers have full citizenship status based on different criteria from men and from other women in that they have a direct relation with the state; it is insofar as this is conflated with the citizenship of wives, which is undecidable between a direct and an indirect relation, that the status of women in their specific difference from men is inferior. In the next section we shall look at how second-wave feminism has tried to deal with this status, mainly by campaigning for the individualisation of benefits and aiming to establish a direct relation between the state and women who are wives. Campaigns directly aimed at gaining recognition of women's specific capacities and responsibilities have not figured so prominently, although it will be argued, the recognition of women's citizenship rights as carers does have radical potential.

SECOND-WAVE FEMINISM AND LIBERAL-DEMOCRACY

This section will look at the relationship between post-war liberal-democracy and second-wave feminism. It is a relationship that is difficult to describe because of the complexity of both liberalism and feminism in the second half of the twentieth-century. Second-wave feminism is often broken down into different theoretical schools so that liberal feminism is distinguished from Marxist, socialist and radical feminisms. It is clear, however, that each has influenced the other, despite antagonisms between different factions of the women's movement (Lovenduski and

Randall, 1993). It is difficult, then, to separate out the influence of liberal feminism on the twentieth-century women's movement generally. Nevertheless, it is reasonable to argue, as the socialist feminist Anne Phillips does, that despite the weakness of an explicitly liberal feminism in Britain, in comparison with the US for example, the gains which second-wave feminism has won for women have largely been in terms of liberal rights (Phillips, 1987a, p. 2). The implication of Phillips' argument is that liberalism is hegemonic, its principles are embedded in social and political practices such that where it has been successful feminism has extended or modified liberalism rather than replaced it. This is the argument that will be pursued here. I take issue, however, with Phillips' reading of liberalism and, on the grounds that liberal rights in the second half of the twentieth century are better described as liberal-democratic rights, I argue that they must be seen as more thoroughly transformative of gender relations than feminists have generally been inclined to suppose.

It should be noted that Phillips' own view of liberalism has changed, and in her recent work on the subject she implies that it may be more flexible, and consequently more useful as a resource for feminism, than she had previously allowed for (see Phillips, 1991, 1993a and 1993b). Her earlier view may, however, be taken as representative of the socialist feminist perspective on liberalism which equates liberalism with equal rights in law. Though Phillips does not explicitly define liberalism as such, she argues that feminist gains have largely been made in these terms, while more revolutionary aims, like building an alternative to the family or 'breaking the hold of patriarchal power', have faltered (Phillips, 1987a, p. 12). She sees this as problematic because gains such as the Equal Pay and Sex Discrimination Acts and equal opportunities policies, though not negligible, are limited in the way that all liberal legislation is limited. First, because it promotes formal rather than substantive equality insofar as it is couched in terms of universal rights and fails to take into account the social and economic circumstances associated with sexual difference which perpetuate inequalities (pp. 7–8). And second, since it is *par excellence* the doctrine that separates the personal from the political sphere, it 'can exempt from political interference the arena in which women are most subordinate and controlled' (p. 13). Phillips' analysis of the limitations of liberalism is, then, clearly related to, and to some extent draws on, the feminist critique of liberalism as masculinist outlined in chapter 2. On the basis of the account of liberalism given in the previous two chapters, it is evident that this critique of liberalism is ahistorical; it is really only applicable to classical liberalism and does not take into account how liberalism has been transformed since the seventeenth century. Liberalism has been democratised and although it is still universalist it need not confine itself to the form of the law to the neglect of social and economic inequalities and sexual difference. Furthermore, the liberal opposition between public and private need not correspond to that between state/civil society and the private domestic sphere. Neither welfare liberalism, which is universalist but not formal, nor Mill's version, in which it is the area of personal freedom around the *individual* that is private rather than the domestic sphere, are captured by this characterisation. Both have been important in the twentieth century. The second-wave feminist use of the language of equal rights has been made within a framework which is better characterised as liberal-democratic than liberal; it embodies previous claims to rights which have extended that language beyond universalism in the form of the law to include political, social and economic rights, including rights in the private domestic sphere. This is not to say that claims to equal rights are *never* merely formal, nor that the privacy of the domestic sphere has not proved resistant to those claims in the twentieth century; it is not that liberalism and feminism have simply progressed together to the point where the rights to liberty and equality originally confined to men in the public sphere of the political have been extended, to women *as* women in the private domestic sphere. The meaning of rights in relation to the public/private opposition and to sexual difference are the outcome of political struggle, not evolution, and can never be finally fixed. But it is important to note the gains that feminism *has* made within a liberal-democratic framework because recognising the way in which it has allowed the politicisation of the private domestic sphere and, to a limited extent, has been able to take sexual difference into account in the public sphere, is important for future feminist strategies of change.

We shall, then, analyse some of the gains second-wave feminism has made in liberal-democratic terms, focusing on the ways in which the opposition between the masculine public sphere of contract and universal rights and the feminine private sphere of care for particular others and natural subordination that was so much in evidence in classical liberalism has been politicised and has become much less distinct. The areas we will look at are those in which the private domestic sphere meets the public sphere of the state and the market. To focus only on these areas is obviously to be highly selective concerning the effects of second-wave feminism, and within the areas I have chosen there is no attempt to include *all* the campaigns in which feminists have been involved. The point is to show how the successes of the movement are better analysed as liberal-democratic, rather than as liberal *tout court*, and the examples I give are intended to be illustrative of this analysis rather than exhaustive.

The first area we will look at is that of equality legislation, in particular that passed to deal with inequalities in the labour market: the Sex Discrimination and Equal Pay Acts of the 1970s. This legislation is universalist – it applies the same standards to all (with some exceptions concerning, for example, protective legislation, maternity leave and retirement age [Carter, 1988, p. 58]) – and in terms of the feminist critique of liberalism as masculinist, it is problematic because it covertly smuggles in a masculine norm under the guise of gender-neutrality. It fails to consider how the sexes continue to be differently constructed, women as primarily responsible for care in the domestic sphere and men as family breadwinners, and simply allows women the formal rights to be like men. Nevertheless, I shall argue that, although the legislation is problematic, it does have the potential to deal with inequalities in the workplace that are associated with this historically constructed sexual difference. Although it is universalist, it is *not* merely formal but is concerned with substantive social and economic inequalities. It is liberal-democratic rather than liberal, more concerned with rights to social and economic resources than with the form of the law.

Equality legislation is described as universalist because it works by *decategorising* gender, by proscribing the use of the category of sex or marital status as a basis for decision or action in the workplace (Frazer and Lacey, 1993, p. 79). The Sex Discrimination Act outlawed discrimination – defined as less favourable treatment on the grounds of sex and including indirect discrimination – where employers specify a criteria for employment that is more likely to be met by one sex than the other and that is not justified by the nature of the work (Coote and Campbell, 1987, p. 119); the Equal Pay Act stipulated that equal pay should be made for work 'that was the same or broadly similar' (p. 116). Criticisms have focused on the implementation of this legislation. The Sex Discrimination Act has proved hard to implement because it requires that individuals prove they have been discriminated against. This is very difficult and even when a case is successful it may not be generalised to cover categories of workers so that discriminatory employment practices are not necessarily changed as a result (Carter, 1988, p. 60). It has not, then, contributed much towards ending the segregation of the labour market that has made the Equal Pay

Act so difficult to implement because women in traditionally 'female' jobs can not directly compare themselves to men in the higher-paid 'male' jobs as doing the same or similar work (p. 58).

These criticisms are undoubtedly pertinent and differentials of segregation and pay have not decreased remarkably since the enactment of this legislation (Carter, 1988, pp. 80–6). Nevertheless, I want to argue that it does have radical potential insofar as its stated aims were made in terms of *substantive* and not simply formal equality, because it is susceptible to interpretations which bring it more into line with those stated aims. Some individual cases of proven sex discrimination, for example, have been generalised to include all those whose situation is like that of the victim on the grounds that members of that group should be able *practically* to meet specified requirements if those requirements are not to be considered discriminatory. For example, it was ruled that the Civil Service age restriction to executive officer grade discriminated against women because, although women *could* work in their twenties – they had the formal right to do so – they were actually less likely to do so because of family responsibilities (Coote and Campbell, 1987, pp. 120–2). In such cases it is women's *actual* ability to meet the requirements of a job, and not just the formal right to that job, that is in question. And in the case of the equal pay legislation, the EEC has ruled that the comparison should be between work of *equal worth*, rather than the same or similar work. Not only does this make it possible to compare the work of men and women in a segregated labour market and so to challenge unequal pay, it also offers a potentially radical challenge to the assessment of feminine work as inferior in skill and importance which has kept wages low. Although there are no standard means of assessing equal worth, some employees have been granted pay rises in the courts on this basis (Coote and Campbell, 1987, pp. 117–19). Again, then, the universal form of the equal pay legislation does not mean that it is necessarily unable to take sexual difference into account; it may be able to do so insofar as it is not merely formal, and rather than abstracting from concrete social and economic circumstances can be made to take these into account in order to bring about substantive equality.

The second area is that of welfare rights, in particular rights to social security benefits. For the most part, second-wave feminist campaigns have aimed at the individualisation of benefits, at establishing a direct relation between the state and *all* categories of citizens, and abolishing the indirect relation with married women. Though it is difficult to characterise such an amorphous movement as second-wave feminism as a whole, it is fair to say that it has been inclined to see the family as inherently oppressive to women and so the tendency has been to campaign for the disaggregation of the income of the family as a unit in order to allow individuals to stand alone, usually with the expectation that they would then recombine in healthier, less oppressive groups (Lovenduski and Randall, 1993, pp. 269–72; Clarke et al., 1987, pp. 146–50).

Success in this respect has been partial. For the most part benefits have been *equalised*, especially since the 1983 EEC directive that they should be, so that with a couple of minor exceptions the contributions and entitlements of women are now formally the same as those of men: married women are now compelled to make the same insurance contributions as men and have the same rights to unemployment and sickness benefits, for example, and they may claim for dependants, including their husbands, if they are sick or unemployed (Carter, 1988, p. 62; Coote and Campbell, 1987, pp. 91–2).[10] Campaigns have, however, been less successful in individualising benefits: the family or household remains the basic unit of assessment for, and payment of, social security benefits. A woman may now be the head of a household and she may even claim benefit for a husband as a dependant but the welfare state continues to construct households as having a single head, rather than as a group of individuals each with their own benefit contributions and entitlements, and few households in which there is a man decide that this should be a woman (Coote and Campbell, 1987, p. 92; Lovenduski and Randall, 1993, p. 50). It might seem, then, that feminist campaigns have won formal universal rights to equality in relation to the welfare state, rights for women to be like men, which have little effect on substantive inequalities because of *actual* differences between the sexes: though the relation of the married or cohabiting woman to the state is *more* direct than previously, it is often still mediated through a man. So, for example, the notorious cohabitation rule, whereby a single woman receiving benefit may be subject to surveillance if it is suspected that she is living with a man who should then support her, remains in place (Coote and Campbell, 1987, p. 92). (Although technically men could be subject to the same harassment, this is virtually unknown.) The welfare state, it seems, continues to construct women as dependent on men and therefore, on the 'difference' feminist account, as less than full citizens.

However, before we conclude that women can only be full citizens insofar as they are like men we must also consider the other aspect of women's citizenship we looked at in the Beveridge Report, the direct relation between mothers and the state. This relation has figured much less prominently in the campaigns of second-wave feminists, in part because of hostility to the family and in particular to women's traditional roles of wife and mother. It is only relatively recently that feminists have (officially) taken a positive view of motherhood, and the celebration of this aspect of women's lives that has emerged in some quarters has had little influence on campaigns aimed at improving the material position of women who are mothers (Lovenduski and Randall, 1993, pp. 277–81). In general, the assumption seems to have been that improved childcare, both in terms of public provision (one of the original demands of the movement) and perhaps also the increased involvement of men, would enable women's work patterns to resemble those of men and so dispense with the need for state recognition of the specific capacities and responsibilities of mothers. At the same time, however, and especially since the rise of neo-liberalism, there has been an understanding of the dangers for women of competing with men in the free market and a recognition of the need to provide for women who have been historically constructed as essentially belonging outside that market, caring for men and children in the home (Clarke et al., 1987, pp. 152–3).

The most prominent example of this understanding was the 'Wages for Housework' campaign of the 1970s which, however, had little support generally in the movement because of the way it appeared to reinforce that traditional construction of women as carers in the home (Clarke et al., 1987, pp. 150–1).[11] Apart from this, campaigns concerned with state recognition of women's status as unpaid carers, and especially mothers, have mainly been *defensive*, concerned that women should not be penalised for their historic dependence, rather than that there should be an extension of provision to women in their traditional roles. So, for example, the 1975 social security legislation which abolished the married woman's National Insurance option, introduced the 'home responsibilities' rule – by which the years any person spent in unpaid care in the home were to be counted towards a pension – and the 'best twenty years' rule – which took only the best 20 years' earnings into account in calculating pensions. The latter has now been dropped – the lifetime's earnings are taken into account (Land, 1991). Similarly, the payment of family allowances to women was successfully defended when it was proposed to redefine it as tax credit payable through men's wage packets (Clarke et al., 1987, pp. 150–1; Coote and Campbell, 1987, p. 92). And it may be in terms of these welfare benefits that are paid to women in return for their contributions as carers that there is the possibility of a form of citizenship which takes the historical specificity of women's position into account. It has been suggested, for example, that child benefit should be increased in order to increase the economic independence of women as mothers, and to ease the financial problems of those increasing numbers of women who are mothers but not wives (Lewis, 1987, p. 97). Another possibility is the new use of 'paid volunteers' to care for the old and sick, where care would previously have been unpaid or institutional (Baldock and Ungerson, 1991). As Jane Lewis argues, it is important that feminist policies should be flexible, not prescriptive; they should increase, not limit the choices women have to make (Lewis, 1987, p. 97). Increasing child benefit and paying individuals to care could have this effect if they were accompanied by the reorganisation of work and the provision of public childcare. They should not used as a way of keeping women in the home, out of the labour market, nor to discourage men from taking responsiblity for the care of children and elderly people. Nor should they be used to control the ethnicity of the population and for this reason they must be granted as a *right* to all citizens; although rights do not guarantee access to resources since they may be, for example, indirectly discriminatory, they are at least easier to monitor and to change than discretionary measures in a racist society. Despite the potential of such policies to reinforce women's traditional domestic position and also the exclusivity of the white nation they do seem to offer a way of establishing social rights for carers in the private sphere which might raise the status of that care as well as mitigating some of the poverty which results from carrying out work which is necessary to the labour market, but not recognised by it. Furthermore, they would do so by building on a form of citizenship which is already, if tenuously, in place. There is widespread support for the universal child benefit already paid directly to mothers (Smart, 1991, p. 163). We shall return to the question of women's citzenship and the difficulties of recognising women's historically specific responsibilities in a pluralist society in the conclusion.

Third, there has been legislation that has explicitly addressed women's subordination in the private domestic sphere. While it is not clear that this legislation can even be seen as liberal on the account of the feminist critique of liberalism as masculinist, it is recognisably a continuation of the so-called permissive legislation of the 1960s which specifically drew on Mill's precept that individual behaviour should be tolerated so long as it did not interfere with others (Weeks, 1981, ch. 13; Lewis, 1992, ch. 2). It was drawn on by the 1957 Wolfenden

Committee Report on Homosexual Offences and Prostitution, for example, which argued that the purpose of the law was to preserve public order and decency and to protect the weak from exploitation, not to impose a pattern of moral behaviour on individuals (Weeks, 1981, pp. 242–3). In effect, permissive legislation constructed *the individual* and his/her own moral decisions as the private sphere, the area into which the law had no right to go, shifting this boundary from the *home* which then became a legitimate, albeit somewhat problematic, sphere of legal regulation.[12] The most impoitant examples of this legislation in terms of women's position in relation to the public/private distinction between the domestic sphere and the state are the 1967 Abortion Act and the 1969 Divorce Act.

Although the Abortion Act was not passed with the explicit intention of restricting the law to give more weight to the decisions of individuals concerning their personal moral behaviour, it did have the effect of redrawing the distinction between public and private around the individual and so of extending rights to women in the domestic sphere. According to the terms of the Act, it is not the individual woman who has the right to decide whether to carry the foetus to term or not, but the medical profession (Lewis, 1992, pp. 57–8). Nevertheless, the Act substantially improved women's rights as individuals, sometimes at the expense of their accepted place as wives and mothers in the conventional family. First, because the rules which doctors use to make their decisions have been very relaxed (Keown, 1988, pp. 163–4). And second, in cases where a woman's decision to terminate a pregnancy has conflicted with the norms of family life, that decision has on occasion been upheld in court. In *Paton* v *UK* 1978 a man appealed to the European Commission on Human Rights after a court refused to prevent his wife from having an abortion. The Commission ruled that the mother's health took priority over that of the foetus in the early stages of pregnancy, and that the mother's right to respect for her private life took priority over the father's right to respect for his private and family life (O'Donovan, 1985, p. 91). While it is true that legal sanctions against abortion have all but been replaced with a different *type* of regulation, that of the medical profession, rather than no regulation at all (and that there is therefore an unevenness in the possibility of securing the necessary permission to have an abortion), nevertheless women have gained a certain right to freedom over their own bodies. This is summed up in the feminist slogan 'a woman's right to choose', which has been used, relatively successfully, to defend abortion legislation against restrictions on the occasions on which it has been threatened (by the Corrie Bill in 1979 and the Alton Bill of 1987) (Lovenduski and Randall, 1993, ch. 7).

The Divorce Reform Act 1969 was much more closely linked to the legal deregulation of individual decisions, which is the distinguishing feature of the permissive legislation. It instituted the principle that courts should no longer be concerned with imputing guilt to either party in a divorce case; they were to deal with marriage only in terms of the financial contract it involved between two individuals. Paradoxically, however, because courts were also concerned to safeguard the welfare of children they were required to intervene more completely and in a more detailed way in what was previously considered the private domestic sphere – in order to arrange custody, access to the children for the non-custodial parent, reasonable maintenance payments, and so on. According to Carol Smart, this divorce legislation involves a new style of legal intervention in domestic matters which is less punitive in orientation but more interventionist. She suggests that as such it was a precursor of legislation passed as a result of feminist campaigns, notably the Domestic Violence Act 1976 and, we could add, the judgment of the 1991 Law Commission that rape in marriage should be criminalised (Smart, 1984, pp. 99–101; Lovenduski and Randall, 1993, p. 330).[13]

Domestic violence would seem to be exemplary of the liberal construction of the private domestic sphere as outside the scope of the law. It was addressed by first-wave feminists and they had some success in getting the law to recognise the need for protection against it (Shanley, 1989, p. 164). However, the protection was never adequate and by the twentieth century domestic violence was again seen as a private matter (O'Donovan, 1985, p. 125). And even following the Domestic Violence Act 1976, which enabled a woman to take out an injunction against a violent partner to prevent him re-entering the home, the law was little used – partly as a result of police reluctance to become involved in private issues and partly because women themselves were often unwilling to give evidence against their assaillants. It was only following public awareness campaigns and the setting up of women's refuges that rates of conviction for domestic violence increased (Lovenduski and Randall, 1993, p. 313). Nevertheless, the legislation did provide for the possibility of making interventions in the domestic sphere for the sake of the protection of the individual and so contributed, though it did not ensure, the extension of democratic rights to women in the home. The recent ruling on marital rape looks similarly difficult to institute. Until very recently, marital rape simply was not a crime; in the terms of a principle first articulated in the eighteenth century, women were held by the law to have given up their right to refuse to have sex with their husbands on marriage (O'Donovan, 1985, p. 119). In 1991 the Law Commission ruled that modern marriage is a partnership of equals and that the usual objections to criminalising marital rape – mainly that there would be problems in verifying evidence – were irrelevant; rape is non-consensual sexual intercourse and women are entitled to refuse intercourse (Lovenduski and Randall, 1993, p. 330). It is not clear yet how the law will be implemented but once again it does provide for the possibility that women may use the language of rights in the private sphere.

Permissive legislation and the feminist legislation that followed it is liberal if by liberal is meant a version close to that inspired by J.S. Mill in which the law and state institutions are to be used to ensure equal rights to individual freedom. It is a version of liberalism which privileges negative freedom over positive, though in practice, like New Liberalism, it aims at a balance between them; it permits intervention in the domestic sphere not just for the sake of the protection of negative liberty but also to promote the well-being – the positive liberty – of citizens, especially children. In terms of the feminist critique of liberalism as masculinist, however, it goes far beyond liberalism because it is used to ensure the rights of women as individuals in the private domestic sphere rather than those of men in the public sphere of the state and civil society in which universal principles are supposed to be applicable. Permissive and feminist legislation embodying the universal principle of the equal right to negative liberty are best understood as liberal-democratic, as extending liberal rights beyond their original male constituency and context in the public sphere to include women in a new and arguably feminine context, that of the private domestic sphere.

In conclusion, then, it is clear that late twentieth-century liberalism is better described as liberal-democratic in comparison with classical liberalism and that it therefore permits the articulation and institution of rights for women both *as* women and as individuals in the several different versions of liberalism that are currently in play. Second-wave feminism has been concerned above all with progressive aspects of Millian and New Liberalism, but in the last 20 years another, much more aggressive version of liberalism has been projected, neo-liberalism, popularly known as Thatcherism, which is in many respects closer to classical liberalism than are the democratised versions we have been discussing in this section. We need, then, to consider whether neo-liberalism has been successful in its hegemonic project to replace these other forms, and in particular how it positions women in relation to the public/private opposition and how successful it has been in instituting this position.

THATCHERISM: NEO-LIBERALISM 'ROLLING BACK THE FRONTIERS OF THE STATE'

In recent years there has been a concerted effort to counteract the extension of democratic rights in the areas we are considering – equality legislation, state provision of welfare and legislation concerning the rights of individuals in the private domestic sphere – popularly known as Thatcherism. Thatcherism has been variously described as a set of policies passed by the government led by Mrs Thatcher (Bulpitt, 1986); as a hegemonic project which set out to destroy the institutions established by the postwar consensus which goes beyond government policies or the pronouncements of Mrs Thatcher herself (Hall, 1983); and as an example of the retreat from the mixed economy and the welfare state which is a product of a worldwide recession (Jessop et al., 1988). It is accepted by all these analyses that Mrs Thatcher has associated herself in numerous statements and speeches with a project that was explicitly against socialism, unions, welfare-state 'scroungers' and the 'permissive society' and for 'rolling back the frontiers of the state' and returning to 'Victorian values' (Hall, 1983). However, this project preceded Thatcher herself: some of the themes of Thatcherism were analysed by Hall et al. before Mrs Thatcher's election as party leader (Hall et al., 1978) and both Conservative and Labour governments attempted to introduce 'Thatcherite' policies to dismantle institutions of the postwar consensus before her election as Prime Minister (Hall, 1983, pp. 9–20; Jones et al., 1991, pp. 49–51). It must, then, be seen as going beyond Mrs Thatcher as a person, or the governments she headed. The problem we shall be addressing here is the extent to which the Thatcherite project, associated, then, only loosely with Mrs Thatcher herself, was actually institutionalised, or even seriously attempted: to what extent has the postwar extension of democratic rights been undermined by Thatcherism?

In addressing this question it is important to recognise that there are inconsistencies in Thatcherism at the level of the rhetoric employed by those associated with it and between the rhetoric and the policies enacted by the Conservative governments since 1979. In part this is because Thatcherism is an uneasy and only partial alliance between various groups and tendencies on the right. Most importantly, the Thatcherite project attempts to unite two different tendencies which have been extremely influential in the writings and speeches of the New Right across the industrialised world (Levitas, 1986, p. 1). First, neo-liberalism or *laissez-faire* economism informed by readings of Adam Smith, Friedrich Hayek and Milton Friedman. This is sometimes taken also to imply libertarianism, or the need for minimal restrictions on individuals generally (Gamble, 1986, pp. 30–1). And second, neo-conservatism or authoritarianism, which values hierarchy and order, opposes the 'permissive society' and sees the patriarchal family as the basis of order (Lovenduski and Randall, 1993, pp. 33–5; Hall, 1983, pp. 29–30; Levitas, 1986). This second tendency is well disposed towards 'moral crusaders' campaigning on behalf of the traditional family – against abortion and sex education (seen as increasing illegitimacy), for example – but they do not always get the support they expect from the Conservative Party. Although concern with the 'permissive society' has been a feaure of Conservative Party rhetoric, concrete proposals for moral change have rarely figured in its manifestos or electoral campaigns (Durham, 1991, pp. 132–6). This is probably becasue they are seen as electorally unpopular and also because their demands are in tension with libertarian tendencies of the New Right. Libertarianism is not generally dominant in the Conservative Party (Gamble, 1986, pp. 46–7), but on occasion it may be significant. So, for example, Norman Tebbit's speeches in the mid-1980s to the effect that collectivist policies were not the sole cause of the nation's ills and that 'The effect of those policies have been dramatically worsened by the onset of the politics of the permissive society' did not meet with universal approval in the Conservative Party itself. Some maintained that personal matters were the responsibility of the individual and not of government (Durham, 1991, pp. 132–4). Furthermore, although the value of the traditional family has featured in Thatcherite rhetoric there has been no outright attack on feminism and very little legislation explicitly directed at reinstituting it. Despite the notorious statement of Patrick Jenkins, then Secretary of State for Social Services, that 'If the Good Lord had intended us to have equal rights to go out to work, he wouldn't have created man and woman' (quoted in Gardiner 1983, p. 195), and despite many other remarks to the effect that family values are women's values 'because women bear the children and create and run the home' (Mrs Thatcher, quoted in Segal, 1983, p. 208) on the part of Mrs Thatcher and her ministers, Thatcherism has made little attempt to revoke equal opportunities polices or to push women back into the domestic sphere

(Segal, 1983; Campbell, 1987, p. 159; Barrett and McIntosh, 1991, pp. 12–13; Lovenduski and Randall, 1993, pp. 40–5). In part this is because of the influence of feminism generally. As Bea Campbell puts it, 'the mid-1970s equality legislation . . . transformed the parameters within which Conservative sexual and familial politics could move' (Segal, 1983, pp. 213–14; Campbell, 1987, p. 160). And it is also because of its influence within the Conservative Party itself, where women have been divided between those who want the government to introduce economic policies to encourage mothers to stay at home with their children, and those who demand policies to further women's advancement in the workplace (Campbell, 1987, pp. 151–65).

In respect of policies aimed specifically at women, then, democratic rights in the private domestic sphere and in the labour market have proved resistant to the Thatcherite project. However, it has gone some way towards reprivatising the domestic sphere as a product of its neo-liberal economic policies (Segal, 1983, p. 209; Waylen, 1986; Barrett and McIntosh, 1991, p. 12). The neo-liberal project of 'rolling back the frontiers of the state' strongly implies the classical liberal view that the private domestic sphere is a special place for the care of children and dependent adults who cannot care for themselves. This is implied in the case of children, insofar as there is practically no state provision of childcare (though this is not new to Thatcherism) (Lovenduski and Randall, 1993, p. 50), and it is explicitly argued for where there has been state provision of care for the sick and elderly, which is now being withdrawn. Speaking to the Women's Royal Voluntary Service at their Annual Conference in 1981, Mrs Thatcher said, 'The voluntary principle is very important for reasons which are far beyond economics.' Earlier in the speech she had said, 'in the end real neighbourliness and understanding care comes from those who choose to do it' (quoted in Land, 1983, p. 11). 'Real' care is here associated with free care, in the sense of not being paid *and* choosing voluntarily to do it, in an implicit opposition to the paid, and therefore presumably grudgingly performed and unreal, care of the public sector. Again, in a government document on the care of the elderly from the same year, it is argued that:

> Whatever level of public expenditure proves practicable and however it is distributed, the primary sources of support and care for elderly people are informal and voluntary. These spring from the personal ties of kinship, friendship and neighbourhood. They are irreplacable. It is the role of public authority to sustain and where

necessary, develop – but never to displace – such support and care.
Care in the community must increasingly mean care by the community.
(quoted in Lewis, 1992, p. 30)

The private domestic sphere of personal, unpaid, 'real' care is opposed
to the public sphere of money and authority, in which 'real' care can
not be provided. This almost duplicates the nineteenth-century separation of spheres but for one important difference; in the nineteenth century it was *women's* place in the private that guaranteed its integrity in
opposition to the public, whereas in the late twentieth century women
are much more difficult to place in this way.

To begin with, as I stated above, consecutive Conservative governments have made little attempt at polices specifically designed to force
women out of work in the paid labour market and back into their traditional feminine roles in the home.[14] The nearest government policies
have come to forcing women back into the home was in 1980 when a
woman's entitlement to return to work following maternity leave was
made dependant on her having worked for the same employer for at
least two years; the legislation was successfully overturned in the courts
(Lovenduski and Randall, 1993, p. 48). The British government also
held out longer than any other against the European ruling that equal
pay should be granted for work of equal value; an extremely important ruling, as we have seen, because of the possibility it allows of
making comparisons between men's and women's work in a highly
segregated labour market (Campbell, 1987, p. 205). But Conservative
governments have made no attempt to repeal equal opportunities policies already in place, and although the Equal Opportunities Commission was under threat for a while that too has been permitted to remain
(Lovenduski and Randall, 1993, p. 46).

Furthermore, Conservative governments have left intact most of the
legislation which, in the past decades, has extended the sphere of the
state into the home and redrawn the opposition between public and
private *within* the domestic sphere, around the individual. In some cases
it has even extended this legislation. Divorce was made easier to obtain; the time bar for obtaining a divorce was reduced from three years
to one year in 1984 (Douglas, 1990, p. 414). And in 1987 legislation
was passed which outlawed the distinction between the fathers of
'legitimate' and 'illegitimate' children; for the purposes of the law the
distinction was no longer to be considered valid (pp. 417–18). Personal relationships and individual moral decisions are again in this
legislation ruled out of bounds for the law.

In the area of welfare rights, legislation has been passed which goes some way towards meeting feminist demands for the disaggregation of individuals' incomes and outgoings. It was a Conservative government which passed the Social Security Act 1986 permitting a woman to count as the head of household for the purposes of collecting Income Support, albeit under pressure from the EEC (Lovenduski and Randall, 1993, p. 46), and in 1989 separate taxation of husbands and wives was introduced allowing individuals who are married a degree of privacy and independence concerning their incomes (p. 49). Such policies are in line with the rhetoric of Thatcherism, which seeks to replace the Beveridgean model of social rights with the idea of a partnership between the individual and the state in which there is a 'stronger emphasis on individual provision than hitherto' (quote from DSS Green Paper, in Smart, 1991, p. 166). Not unexpectedly, then, despite the rhetoric concerning the importance of care in the private domestic sphere, Thatcherism has not sought to extend citizenship rights to women *as* women, in their traditional capacity as unpaid carers. On the contrary, there is resistance to such rights as already exist on the grounds that they undermine the role of the male breadwinner and contribute to the break-up of the family (Smart, 1991, p. 160). In line with the neo-conservative vision of the traditional nuclear family, but more importantly, with neo-liberal economic policies of 'rolling back the frontiers of the state', child benefit, though not abolished as has been proposed, has been frozen by successive governments (Johnson, 1990, p. 45) and the universal maternity grant has been replaced by a means-tested maternity needs payment (Smart, 1991, p. 166). On the other hand, again under pressure from Europe, the Invalid Care Allowance, previously payable only to single persons caring for the disabled, was extended to married and cohabiting women (pp. 55–6).

Thatcherism rhetoricises a public/private opposition that is reminiscent both of classical liberalism and New Liberalism. In both cases the opposition between the public sphere of the state and market and the private domestic sphere is made simultaneously possible and impossible by the status of women as both like and different from men. Thatcherism constructs women along neo-liberal lines as individuals with the universal rights of individuals to compete, unhampered by government restrictions, in the free market; at the same time it positions them as wives and mothers, economically dependent on male breadwinners and unselfish in their capacity as the unpaid carers of men and children in the private domestic sphere. The public sphere of the minimal state and free market of neo-liberalism requires the private domestic sphere of unselfish care to which it is opposed. And it is the undecidability of women as simultaneously identical to men and different from them that makes the opposition between public and private both possible and ultimately impossible. Thatcherism is similar in this respect to Locke's classical liberalism. They are also closely related insofar as the state is minimal for both and it is the universal form of the law that makes it just, not substantive rights to social and economic equalities. With regard to the public/private opposition, Thatcherism is also similar to New Liberalism as it was instituted in the National Insurance scheme of the welfare state. In both cases, women are undecidable between the individuals of liberalism with rights to liberty and equality, however minimal, guaranteed by the state, and women with specific characteristics which put them outside that entitlement. Millian liberalism is, as we have seen, somewhat different: both women *and* men are undecidable between public and private, and the distinction between them can be made within the domestic sphere; it is not equivalent to that between the state and civil society and the home. However, the liberal-democratic extension of rights to women *as* women, however tenuous, in the public sphere of the labour market and the welfare state and to women as individuals in the private domestic sphere that we have examined in this chapter, has made policies designed to institute a 'pure' opposition between public and private difficult to pursue. It is politically imprudent for some, and unthinkable for others, to try to force women into a position of dependency and subordination in the private domestic sphere. This position has never been unequivocal in any version of liberalism, as we have seen, and following the changes we have traced, including changes resulting from feminist activity, it is a good deal more difficult to discern in liberal-democratic practices today. The undecidability of women between the individual of the universal liberal principles of liberty and equality and the naturally caring woman of the domestic sphere has been opened up by the liberal-democratic practices of the late twentieth century and this has complicated the institution of the public/private oppostion itself. Furthermore, this undecidability is now very difficult to close down.

Conclusion:
Feminist Decisions

This study has shown how liberalism, in three different historically specific but overlapping forms, has been relatively successful in establishing forms of hegemony in modern Britain. It has taken the categories of liberalism as constitutive of contemporary social practices, notably of women's undecidable position in relation to the crucial public/private distinctions now operative between the domestic sphere and the state/civil society and between the individual and society.

In order to see liberalism in this way, as constitutive of social practices, we have situated it in a political theory that goes beyond liberalism, that takes liberalism as its object: the theory of hegemony. The point is not, then, to make a straightforward defence of liberalism against its feminist critics by showing that it is not as they describe it, though that is one aspect of the project, but rather to show how liberalism, although limited, has been, and can be useful for feminism. The theory of hegemony is a theory of *le politique*, of politics which institutes new social forms, including forms of liberalism itself. On this view liberalism is not rigidly fixed in the categories and oppositions of classical liberalism, as feminist critics seem to suppose – the individual is not necessarily masculine, the private domestic sphere is not necessarily opposed to the state, women are not necessarily recognised only as dependants in the public sphere, and so on. Rather, because there are no transcendental guarantees which could definitively secure the meaning of the social forms of liberalism, its categories and oppositions are always open to contestation and can only be partially fixed in hegemonic projects.

Neither is it being claimed that all feminists need is liberalism. Although I have traced the close relation between liberalism and feminism since the seventeenth century and the way in which feminism has used liberal categories counter-hegemonically, this is not to say that feminism has thought only within its terms. Manifestly this is not so since it is always possible, albeit with a certain amount of strain, to classify feminist theory otherwise: as Marxist, socialist, radical and now as poststructuralist and postmodern. Furthermore, feminists have politicised social practices in ways that would be difficult, if not impossible, to identify from a liberal perspective. This is true, for example, of some sexual practices which feminists have problematised and which liberals of all descriptions would see as matters of individual choice: what is now called sexual harassment and the use of pornography are practices of this kind (Frazer and Lacey, 1993, p. 211). Liberalism is not to be seen as a social theory which can be used to identify instances of gender inequality.

What is being claimed is that feminism has had a close relationship with liberalism from the beginning and that it has been able to use it in distinctively feminist ways because of the undecidability of the category women in liberal political thought. For liberalism, whether that of Locke, Mill or Beveridge, the term 'women' is always undecidable between woman, the inferior term of the binary opposition between the sexes, and 'human' or 'man' the superior term, the bearer of the 'universal' liberal rights to freedom and equality. This undecidability is, in classical and New Liberalism, constitutive of the public/private distinction which is central to the tradition. We have seen how useful this constitutive undecidability has been to feminists campaigning both for women's rights to do things that traditionally only men have been able to do and also in creating a space in the liberal polity for the recognition of women's specific capacities and the rights that should accompany those capacities. We have also seen how the undecidability of 'women' is now open as a result of feminist activity, such that there is an unwillingness on the part of the neo-liberal contenders for hegemony to close it off by deciding for women as carers in the private domestic sphere, or, for that matter, as ungendered individuals competing in the public sphere.

The question is, then, how to proceed from here given that, despite the gains feminism has made, there is still considerable inequality between the sexes? Although this study has presented what might seem to some as rather an optimistic account of feminism's successes, I do not mean to suggest that women are now on an equal footing with men as a result of the changes it has undoubtedly brought about. On the contrary, I would agree with Esther Breitenbach's useful distinction between autonomy and equality. While women are now more free than they were a generation ago insofar as they are more able to control reproduction, to escape from violent or unhappy relationships and so on, in comparison with men they are still in a position of inequality – access to opportunities and resources is still extremely restricted for women, especially those with children (Lovenduski and Randall, 1993, p. 24). The problem is how to understand this continuing inequality, and specifically in the context of this study, how it is related to the principles of liberal-democracy with which feminists have tried to change it: what strategies should feminists pursue to try to eliminate it? On the basis of the history of liberal social and political institutions, and feminism's relation to the undecidability of women embedded in them, there are at least three possibilities.

The first is that feminism could decide definitively for women as like men and therefore to be treated on strictly identical terms. This is the position usually associated with liberalism. It has probably never been taken very seriously in Britain, though it has been adopted in the US. In Britain, although, as we have seen, early second-wave feminists were inclined to minimise differential treatment of the sexes, to emphasise women's identity as ungendered individuals, the influence of socialism with its tradition of collective provision and its emphasis on the determining nature of social structures meant that they were wary of taking the approach too far. Although androgyny was the ultimate aim, most saw women's historical position in the family as requiring 'special treatment' in the short term at least (Bacchi, 1990, pp. 259–61).

The androgynous approach is now thoroughly discredited. As the feminist critiques of liberalism argue, it leaves the masculine norm intact and where women do not fit that norm because of their embodied difference and the associations that have accompanied it, they are at a disadvantage. For example, it makes no sense to defend the right to abortion in gender-neutral terms, and to do so may obscure the extent to which it is an issue of sexual equality (Okin, 1991).

Second, feminism could decide for women as fundamentally different from men – whether biologically or for social reasons – and argue that therefore women have a particular contribution to make which should be recognised. Along these lines, Nell Noddings argues that the caring that is associated with women could provide the basis for a reformed society in which morally legitimate action would be guided by feelings of connectedness to others and the fostering of relationships rather than by the detached, universal ethical principles which have perpetuated so much violence in the name of what is right (Noddings, 1984). In such a world Noddings suggests that women, and presumably, by extension, what women do, would be less likely to be judged inferior (p. 3); in fact, we might suppose that they would be considered *superior*. Although, like Gilligan on whose work she draws, Noddings repeatedly states that the ethic of care is not exclusive to women, that men can and do share it, she nevertheless insists that it is to be seen as 'classically' feminine – rooted in receptivity, relatedness and responsiveness (p. 2) – and a very traditional style of mothering is taken as the paradigm of caring activity throughout her work.

The problem with this proposal is that it is essentialist. It sees the identity of women as something which can be captured in a single description, a single list of attributes. Women, or at least the 'feminine' with which they are associated, are characterised as they are for liberalism, by their capacity for the love and care of particular others to whom they feel connected. The feminist critique of essentialism is well established: there is no single list of attributes which could capture all the aspects of women's varied, and continually changing, identities. Some women would not recognise themselves as such in Noddings' regime. Furthermore, to adopt such a traditional definition of what it is to be a woman seems more likely to reinforce existing gender inequality than to transform it. And from the point of view of the history of liberalism, since, as we have seen, it has been the undecidability of women between their characterisation as ungendered individuals and as caring feminine women that has been most productive, it would seem to be counterproductive to insist that women are, and must be, nothing but women.

Third, then, feminism could simply refuse to decide at all. Having opened up the undecidability of the category 'women', we could simply refuse to close it down again by making a decision one way or the other. This is Derrida's preferred strategy. Asked to comment on 'woman's place', a rather contentious way of asking how women have been, and perhaps by implication should be, positioned in the philosophical discourse of the West, he answers:

> in my view *there is no one place for woman*. . . . The joyous disturbance of certain women's movements, and of some women in particular, has actually brought with it the chance for a certain risky turbulence in the assigning of places within our small European space. . . . Is one then going to start all over again making maps, topographies, etc.? Distributing sexual identity cards.
>
> (Derrida, 1991, pp. 442–3; author's emphasis)

On this account, any description or redescription of what woman 'is', any decision for or against women as like or different from men, will close off the possibilities of escaping the binary opposition between the sexes. For Derrida the possibility of a multiplicity of sexed identities is opened up by the deconstructive reading of women as an identity that cannot be fully occupied since, like any other apparently self-present category, it is always shot through with undecidability, with the impossibility of fully constituting itself. According to Derrida, a similar opening up is now happening across the social field as a result of the activities of the feminist movement (or rather, of *some* of its activities, since, as we have seen, feminism may also work to reinstate an essentialist identity of women) which disrupts the apparent self-evidence of women as a category and refuses it as an identity. Feminism has opened up the undecidability of women and we should now work to keep it open, rather than closing it down again.

However, as Derrida himself recognises, it may not be enough for feminism to confine itself to disrupting sexed identities where the object is to change the way in which women continue to be positioned, not in one place certainly – no longer 'in the home' – but nevertheless in second place to men across a range of different social practices. Once we take account, he says, of 'the real conditions in which women's struggles develop on all fronts (economic, ideological, political)' we have to recognise that:

> These conditions often require the preservation (within shorter or longer phases) of metaphysical presuppositions [that is, that woman has *a* position which she occupies fully, without the disruption of undecidability] that one must (and knows already that one must) question in a later phase – or another place – because they belong to the dominant system that one is deconstructing on a practical level.
>
> (Derrida, 1991, pp. 445–6)

So we return to the question of the decision. Deconstruction of the undecidability of the identity of women can never be enough for feminism; politics – *le politique* – requires both the opening up of undecidability and also the moment of decision, of deciding for the meaning of an ultimately impossible identity. Feminists have to make practical decisions in the context of hegemonic projects aimed at improving women's social, economic and political position. In the liberal-democracy we are concerned with here, feminists have, on occasion, to decide for women as the same or as different from men.

Given, then, that sometimes feminists have to decide for the identity of women as opposed to opening up its undecidability, how should we proceed? Can we decide *for* women without falling into the trap of essentialism and without closing off the very possibility of a more radical displacement of rigid gender identity? Following Drucilla Cornell's rethinking of deconstruction and feminism, we can decide for the identity of women without becoming entangled in essentialism if we see that decision as involving a re-metaphorisation of the term 'women', rather than the description of a real group of people. We must, she argues, be careful to distinguish between essence and properties: 'essence' presupposes direct access to the thing itself while metaphor works by transferring the properties of one thing to another which is 'like' the first. It is always prescriptive – since we have no access to the thing itself we assign it properties.

In this respect any description of woman is risky, it risks, as Derrida argues, assigning her to her proper place (Cornell, 1991, p. 31). The risk must nevertheless be taken, Cornell argues. On her view, the re-metaphorisation of women is necessary because undoing the metaphysical opposition of sexual difference requires more than simply denying it – it requires the 'overturning' of the hierarchy of the opposed terms. Here she is following the Derridean method of deconstruction, the 'marching order' outlined in chapter 1: the inferior term of a binary opposition must be privileged over the superior term before the logic that holds them together can be dismantled. This 'overturning' is not a temporal moment, it is not something that can be done once and for all, because oppositions continually reassert themselves: deconstruction is interminable. According to Cornell, then, we must continually affirm the identity of women. Without an affirmation to overturn the hierarchy, she argues, it is as if the opposition had *already* been deconstructed, as if we had *already* escaped the opposition of sexual difference in a new multiplicity of sexed, gender identities. There is multiplicity, but there is also the systematic subordination of women, and it is this that must be dismantled (pp. 95–6).

Against Derrida, Cornell argues that the affirmation of women need not involve the preservation of metaphysical presuppositions, it need not involve the presupposition that there is a self-present identity of women waiting to be described. The description, and continual redescription, of women should not be seen as a representation of what women truly and authentically are, what they are in essence. Language is performative, it produces what it names, rather than naming something outside itself; the continual re-metaphorisation of women should therefore be seen as constitutive, as acting on us as 'genderised subjects'. If we recognise the constitutive power of metaphor, we can keep the identity of women relatively open whilst affirming that identity in order to reverse the hierarchy of the binary opposition of sexual difference and make a genuinely new multiplicity of gender identities available (Cornell, 1991, pp. 100–1).

Cornell is evidently concerned to carry out this deconstruction of sexual difference in practice for the sake of equality, and not simply, say, for the sake of celebrating femininity and difference. At least, this is presumably her aim since she is arguing for a reversal of the binary opposition of sexual difference in order to allow for multiplicity without subordination. She does not, however, make the priority of equality clear. Similarly, she argues that her proposals allow feminism to take into account differences within the category 'women', as well as the affirmation of their difference from men. Precisely because re-metaphorisation does not involve the description of a true essence, but the description of one thing as 'like' another, it can allow for both sameness and differences between women. The re-metaphorisation of women can allow for the description of the embodied specificity of white women, for example, as different from that of black women in some respects but as significantly alike in others (Cornell, 1991, pp. 194–6). Again, Cornell assumes, but does not state, the aim of equality: she assumes that it would be racist, it would contribute to the material advantage of white women over black, either if women were all described as alike, or if black and white were described as completely different.[1]

In order to draw out the implications of the centrality of equality to the feminist project I suggest that we situate Cornell's proposals concerning the re-metaphorisation of women in the context of the project of radical democracy theorised by Ernesto Laclau and Chantal Mouffe. What Laclau's and Mouffe's theory of radical democracy makes clear is the *aim* of a re-metaphorisation which would allow for the practical deconstruction of the binary opposition between the sexes and for identity and difference within the category women. The project of radical democracy aims to link together elements – identities and demands made on behalf of them – constructed in previously unconnected contexts across the social field, in order to secure a hegemonic formation which would achieve the maximum degree of equality for all (Laclau and Mouffe, 1985, pp. 181–4). The universality of this project does not presuppose homogeneity and the interchangeability of individuals. It is a universality which allows for difference: each identity is linked in equivalence, in Cornell's terms it is re-metaphorised as like the others, but while it is modified by these links, it retains a distinct difference from them (pp. 181–3).

On the theory of radical democracy, there are two important reasons for explicitly taking equality as the aim of the feminist project. First, the principle of universal equality provides a common point of reference around which different projects – those of anti-racism and anti-sexism in this case – can be linked. According to the theory of radical democracy, the universal principles of equality, and of liberty (which we will deal with below), provide the common language in terms of which all contemporary political projects are constructed. This is because they are extensions of the principles actually embedded in the social and political practices of liberal-democracy:

> If one considers the liberal democratic tradition to be the main tradition of behaviour in our societies, one can understand the extension of the democratic revolution and development of struggles for equality and liberty in every area of social life as being the pursuit of these 'intimations' present in liberal democratic discourse.
>
> (Mouffe, 1993a, p. 16)

Second, it is important that the explicit aim of the feminist project should be the equality of *all* women if some are not to gain ground at the expense of others. In fact, as the theory of radical democracy makes clear, the important issue cannot only be that of equality for women; it must be that of equality for all. The institutionalisation of equality for women must be a collective project: it involves the transformation of contemporary social and political practices and democratic rights can only be exercised insofar as they are recognised collectively (Laclau and Mouffe, 1985, pp. 184–5). But this means that the feminist project – which aims for equal rights for women – must be part of a wider project, that of radical democracy – which is concerned with equal rights for all, including men. In this respect the continual re-metaphorisation of women Cornell advocates must allow for the drawing of equivalences between men and women, as well as for the affirmation of women's specificity. The most immediately obvious of these equivalences would seem to be in terms of the identities of class, race, ethnicity, region, and so on. Without the construction of such equivalences there can be no thoroughgoing transformation of women's subordination to men.

Situating Cornell's proposals for the re-metaphorisation of women in the context of Laclau's and Mouffe's theory of radical democracy also allows us to consider the importance of the other universal principle of liberal-democracy, that of liberty. Cornell does not make any concrete proposals in *Beyond Accommodation* as to how the affirmation of women would work in the liberal-democratic institutions with which we are concerned in this study: in *la politique*, in social policy and law, as well as in *le politique*, in what we might call political culture. Given, however, that on her position social and political practices should affirm the specificity of women in order to equalise the position between the sexes, important issues would presumably include the revalorisation of 'women's' work in the public and the private domestic spheres, the state recognition of women's capacity to become pregnant, give birth, breast-feed, perhaps even the affirmation of women as the mothers of young children for whom those children tend to be a primary concern, women's responsibilities for the care of others generally, and so on. Policies for women might then include, and, as we saw in the section on the feminist use of liberalism in the previous chapter, to some extent they already do include, the right to leave the paid labour market for several years without being penalised in terms of employment opportunities, pension rights, and so on. They might also include the state recognition of mothering as a contribution to the social fund similar to that made in cash by paid workers. However, this affirmation of women's specificity, though necessary for equality, poses dangers for individual freedom. And to the extent that it does so, it also risks a consolidation of the rigid binary opposition between the sexes that Cornell is specifically concerned to combat. The danger is that those identified, and self-identified, as women will be expected to conform to the metaphors of women used to describe them; they will be expected to conform to expectations of what women are 'like'. If, however, we rethink Cornell's proposals as one aspect of a project of radical democracy, we may be able to avoid these consequences.

According to the theory of radical democracy, universal liberty and equality can never actually be achieved: the attainment of complete equality and freedom for all is the horizon for which political movements aim in liberal-democracies and so it can never, by definition, be reached (Laclau and Mouffe, 1985, pp. 190–1). Furthermore, universal equality and freedom is impossible because there is an intrinsic tension between the two principles. They are similar in that both involve the collective recognition of rights, without which rights can not be exercised. But they are different insofar as equality always invokes a collective identity on behalf of which it is claimed. There is no possible institutionalisation of equality except on behalf of a social or political identity, and such identities always, at least in principle, describe a number of persons who could conform to that description. On the other hand, the demand for liberty does not necessarily invoke a collective identity on Laclau's and Mouffe's account; it can be claimed on behalf of the individual (p. 184). There is, then, an irreducible tension between the demands for equality on behalf of collectivities, and the paradoxical demands, paradoxical because obviously they can only be made and sustained collectively, on behalf of individuals to be free of collectively imposed restraints, to be self-determining (Mouffe, 1993b).

Individual rights to freedom must be recognised if the hierarchical binary opposition between the sexes is to be displaced. The problem is that to affirm the specificity of women, especially in law and social policy which may be particularly constraining in comparison with less rigidly institutionalised representations, risks trapping individuals in a sexed identity with which they may not fully identify. In fact, it is impossible to identify completely with any identity since, as we have seen, identity can never be fully constituted; it can never be fully present. Since identities can never achieve self-presence, no one can ever fully 'be' an identity. This is how we should understand the individual. It is not a 'natural' or a pre-social human being, as Locke or Mill would have it; it is a possibility that is constantly thrown up by the necessary failure of identity (Laclau, 1990, pp. 43–5). And if there are to be changes in the possibility of living sexual difference, if the hegemonic binary opposition between the sexes is to be displaced, it is important to recognise that positions made ready in that opposition cannot be fully occupied. It is the failure of completion of identities that makes contestation both possible and necessary. Another way of putting this would be to say that no one is ever *just* a man or a woman, though they are (almost) always that too (with the exception of hermaphrodites). This is not only because they are always at the same time other social identities but because every failure to occupy social identities is irreducibly particular, unique in its failure fully to 'be' normal.

It is this uniqueness which is best described in terms of the liberal theory of individuality. As William Connolly puts it:

> A theory of liberal individuality . . . comprises a range of conduct that is distinctive, stretches the boundaries of identity officially given to the normal self, reveals artifice in established standards of normality by superseding or violating them, and brings new issues into public life through resistances, eccentricities, refusals, or excesses that expose a series of contestable restraints built into fixed conventions.
>
> (Connolly, 1992, p. 75)

Connolly here is writing specifically on the liberal theory of George Kateb, but this is not far from J.S. Mill's view of individuality, which although bound up in an unacceptable teleological theory of the common good and social development led him, as we have seen, to make a vigorous defence of individual freedom. Compare Mill:

> It is not by wearing down into uniformity all that is individual in themselves but by calling it forth, within the limits imposed by the rights and interests of others, that human beings become a noble and beautiful object of contemplation; and as the works partake the character of those who do them, by the same process human life also becomes rich, diversified and animating, furnishing more abundant aliment to high thoughts and elevating feelings. . . . In proportion to the development of his individuality, each person becomes more valuable to himself, and is therefore capable of being more valuable to others.
>
>   (Mill, 1989a, p. 63)

The liberal theory of individuality is to be distinguished from liberal *individualism*, which, as we have seen, presupposes the interchangeability of individuals. The liberal theory of individuality affirms, on the contrary, the uniqueness of the individual; it is the impossibility of substituting one individual for another that must be taken into account in liberal social and political institutions. And it is only insofar as every individual is unique that universal principles are to be applied to all alike. (See Connolly, 1992, pp. 73–81 for discussion of a similar distinction between liberal individuality and liberal individualism.)

To protect individual freedom, law and social policy should be couched in terms which allow for individuality. Social and political practices should affirm women but they should also allow for the possibility that individuals may not 'fit' the metaphors used to institute these practices. For example, sex discrimination laws should allow for differences between men and women in terms of child-bearing, child-rearing, and so on, but they should also prohibit discrimination between individuals on the basis of their sex. That is, no individual should be expected to conform entirely to their sexed identity. This is just, given that individuality must always exceed sexual difference. But it is also important if the possibility that one day the binary opposition of sexual difference will give way to a multiplicity of sexed identities is to be realised, since only where it is acknowledged that the categories of that opposition are not fully occupied can there be contestation and change. Only where there is room for the individuality that exceeds the binary opposition of sexual difference, as well as the affirmation of women's specificity needed to overturn it, can there be a genuine opening up of new possibilities, a repositioning of the sexes that goes beyond the hierarchy currently instituted.

This returns us to the terms of the problem which has been the focus of this study, within which are now trying to address the question of what feminism should do about the continuing subordination of women: the constitutive undecidability of women in liberalism. This conclusion has rejected three possibilities proposed by feminists in recent years: to decide for the identity of women as identical to men; to decide for the identity of women as different from men; and not to decide at all, simply to leave open the undecidability that has been opened up by feminists in the last 25 years. It has followed Drucilla Cornell in arguing that there must be a decision for women, women's specificity must be affirmed for the sake of equality between the sexes, but that this affirmation should be seen as a description that is *productive* of women's identity, rather than as a true description of the 'essence' of women. In response to the dangers of Cornell's own proposal, however, it has been situated as just one aspect of the wider project of radical democracy which aims at the impossible institution of universal equality and liberty. The emphasis on individual liberty in radical democracy, however, an emphasis which it derives from the tradition of liberalism on which it draws, again opens up the question of undecidability. What the emphasis on individuality makes clear is that, although, as Cornell argues, feminism must on occasion decide for women *as* women, it must affirm the specificity and the value of the attributes of women, on other occasions it must decide for women *as like men*, as ungendered individuals who are constantly produced in their uniqueness by the impossibility of fully occupying social categories. This is not in contradiction with Cornell's thesis, though it does change its emphasis. Where Cornell proposes only a re-metaphorisation of women as like women, I am suggesting that we also need a re-metaphorisation of women as like men, who are in turn re-metaphorised as like the ungendered individuals of late twentieth-century liberal-democratic practice.

In a sense, then, the conclusion is that feminism must work to keep open the liberal undecidability of women. It should keep open the undecidability it has opened up in liberal-democratic practices: between women as individuals, masculine in classical liberalism, situated only in the public sphere and interchangeable with other masculine individuals in the universal principles of liberty and equality, but ungendered in late twentieth-century liberal-democracy and possible also in the private domestic sphere; and the embodied, caring, feminine woman, in classical liberalism confined to the private domestic sphere and outside the scope of the universal principles of liberty and equality, but now taken up in them in some cases, precisely because the (ultimately impossible) realisation of those principles requires the recognition of women's specificity.

At the turn of the twenty-first century, then, feminists do have to decide between these two possibilities, in order, paradoxically, to displace the hierarchical binary opposition on which they were historically founded. In this study we have traced the disruption of this opposition, but the hierarchy remains. Nevertheless, although decisions have to be made, they should be confined, as they have generally been throughout the history of feminism's relationship with liberalism, to practical problems in determinate situations. Feminism should adopt Cornell's proposals to affirm women on a small scale, always with a view to increasing equality and to fostering links with other subordinate identities. It should refuse the definitive decision that women *are* women, *are* unlike men, which characterised classical liberalism and which seems also to be suggested by the feminist critique of liberalism as masculinist. As well as affirming the identity of women on some occasions, it should be nimble enough, as it has been in the past, to decide, on other occasions, for women as ungendered individuals. Feminism must make decisions, but it must also work, as it has done since the beginning of modernity, to open and keep open the liberal undecidability of women.

Notes

CHAPTER 1

1. I shall confine the discussion to the question of the formation of concepts in binary oppositions since it is these that concern us in our analysis of liberalism. Deconstruction is not only concerned with binary oppositions, however, though they are certainly one of the most important ways in which philosophy attempts to secure the presence of its key ideas. Concepts also appear in other relations of interdependence – in chains, for example, or as the central predicate of a cluster of predicates (Gasche, 1986, pp. 128–30). Each specific organisation of concepts must be accounted for in a different way, though there are also relations between the different ways of accounting for them (Gasche, 1986, p. 142).

CHAPTER 2

1. In this respect, perhaps, this study may be seen, somewhat paradoxically, as taking a position which more closely resembles that of the feminist critiques of liberalism it criticises than it does those of the rare feminists who argue that feminism simply involves an extension of liberalism's gender-neutral principles. In actual fact, the only feminist I know who takes this position is Janet Radcliffe Richards (Richards, 1982).
2. This approach is controversial among feminist psychoanalytic theorists. The way in which it theorises the social reproduction of femininity and masculinity is seen as a strength because it enables us to understand why women continue to want to mother and men continue to be more or less absent fathers according to the arrangements of contemporary Western society; in other words, it helps us to understand the reproduction of the current conditions of women's subordination. This, it is argued, is not easily explained on the Lacanian account. Once we deny Freud's dictum that 'anatomy is destiny' and focus on how anatomical differences between the sexes are mediated symbolically in the unconscious, there seems to be no good reason why men should adopt a masculine identification in the symbolic order and women a feminine one (DiStefano, 1991, pp. xvi–xv). A similar point is argued in reverse by those who maintain that a Lacanian approach is more useful. It is argued that the importance of psychoanalysis is that it shows how social identities are continually disrupted by the unconscious; it precisely can not be used to describe or explain how the social is reproduced (Rose, 1983).
3. For criticisms of Chodorow's theory, see Rose (1983); Eisenstein (1984, ch. 9); Segal (1987, pp. 134–5); Fraser and Nicholson (1990).
4. There is a good deal of controversy over whether the evidence Gilligan provides in *In a Different Voice* supports the view that women and men

differ in moral orientation and many studies since then have thrown doubt
on whether, if two distinct orientations can actually be clearly identified,
men are more likely to adopt an ethic of justice and women an ethic of
care to deal with moral dilemmas (Broughton, 1983; Kohlberg et al., 1984;
Greeno and Maccoby, 1986; Luria, 1986; Gilligan, 1986; Friedman, 1987a).

CHAPTER 3

1. As noted in chapter 1, Pateman, with Teresa Brennan, has also made a
reading of Hobbes, discussing how women are excluded from the commonwealth in *The Leviathan* (Brennan and Pateman, 1979). Hobbes could
be considered the first liberal in so far as he was the first to elaborate a
model of society around a public/private distinction. His liberalism is, however,
tenuous because the position of this distinction is established by the ruler
rather than by the rights of individuals – it can be redefined by the sovereign at any time for the sake of political order. Generally, political liberalism is seen as holding some rights of private individuals as necessarily
outside the jurisdiction of political society; if they are violated, that society is no longer legitimate. Locke's political philosophy is of this kind and
it is for this reason that he is more easily situated at the origin of liberal
thought than Hobbes. Others who have written on Locke from a feminist
perspective include: Eisenstein (1981); Elshtain (1981, pp. 116–27); Nicholson
(1986, ch. 4); Coole (1988, ch. 4).
2. Having discussed Eve as Adam's double as the recipient of God's gift of
dominion over the world, Locke then goes on to respond to doubts that
'them' in this case means Adam and Eve rather than mankind itself. As he
points out, this argument gives no advantage to Filmer, but rather to himself (Locke, 1960, pp. 196–7). It is at any rate significant that he can only
make this proposal – which obviously suits him very well since it allows
for the unity of mankind in the origin – once he has introduced Eve's
difference as a double into Filmer's origin. He must deal with the possiblity
that 'them' means Adam and Eve, in which case Eve was not so subject to
Adam as to have forfeited the rights of men to the fruits of the earth,
before he can propose that perhaps 'them' means mankind as a whole.
3. It is of course well known that one of Locke's principal objects is to ensure the separation of the bodies which make and execute the law in order
to guard against the abuse of power, and in this respect it may seem somewhat odd to argue that for Locke authority must be unified. However, it is
not this separation of powers that makes the law just for Locke; it is the
unity and universality of the law which makes it legitimate, which gives
the law its authority.
4. The only differences which do exclude individuals from being considered
as identical to every other individual, that is as essentially free and equal,
are differences in the capacity for reason. Those excluded include 'Lunaticks
and Ideots', children not yet grown to maturity, and 'Innocents' and 'Mad-
men' (Locke, 1960, p. 350). The differences which could arise between
husbands and wives obviously do not exhaust the kinds of disagreements
that are possible in the private sphere. Perhaps most obviously, there could

be disagreements between the heads of households in the private sphere. As far as I can see Locke nowhere discusses this problem, except in one short passage where he acknowledges that there are differences between men: of age, virtue or merit which give some precedence over others and of birth, alliance or benefits which may 'subject some . . . to pay an Observance to those to whom Nature, Gratitude or other Respects may have made it due'. However, he immediately goes on to argue that 'in respect to Jurisdiction or Dominion one over the other' these differences are irrelevant, since they do not affect man's natural freedom and equality (Locke, 1960, p. 346). In other words, he immediately subsumes these differences in the identity of mankind under universal law.

5. Interestingly the relation between master and servant is similar in this respect insofar as it is a contractual relationship in the private domestic sphere (Locke, 1960, pp. 365–6). It is, therefore, a private relationship which is regulated by the universal laws of the public sphere. This type of relationship will, of course, be removed from the domestic sphere to become part of civil society – the private sphere of the economy – as capitalism develops. In contrast, the relationship between master and slave is not contractual and is therefore situated entirely in the private sphere; slaves are not part of civil society and are subject to the 'Absolute Dominion and Arbitrary Power of their Masters' (p. 365). Slaves, then, are entirely excluded from the universal principles of Locke's liberalism in a way that women clearly are not.

6. It is not possible to take self-designation as the key here since the term feminism was not used to refer to women campaigning on behalf of women until the late nineteenth century. However, as Carole Pateman points out, the naming of feminist predecessors as such is an important one since not to do so may contribute to the repression of history which has already taken place and which is only now being recovered (Pateman, 1989, p. 15).

CHAPTER 4

1. Other feminist writings on Mill in the 'difference' feminist tradition include: Elshtain (1981, pp. 134–46); DiStefano (1991, ch. 4); Gatens (1991b, ch. 2). His work has also been commented on from a wider feminist perspective: Moller Okin (1980, ch. 9); Eisenstein (1981, ch. 6); Krouse, in Elshtain (1982); Coole (1988, ch. 6).

2. Mill may be seen here as supporting a gendered division of intellectual labour wich gives women the drudgery and men the glory. However, his point is that even without the benefit of education, women are well equipped to act according to practical reason and so there are no good grounds to exclude them from occupations only open to men.

3. Both Bentham and Mill saw a good case for granting women the vote on the grounds that they had interests which conflicted with those of men. However, neither of them developed this argument, apparently on the pragmatic grounds that the public would not consider such radicalism and that to insist on it would jeopardise the more reasonable case for the extension of the franchise to working men (Macpherson, 1977, pp. 36–7 and 40).

4. The ideas feminists themselves developed concerning the power of men and their part in women's subordination were obviously also important. There is a recent radical feminist reinterpretation of first-wave feminism which sees it largely in terms of a struggle against male power, especially male sexual power, rather than against injustice within a liberal frame of reference. See Kent (1990).

5. We are ignoring, then, the important campaigns for education, increased opportunities for single women, the legitimation of roles other than those of wife and mother, and the reform of masculine sexuality (Levine, 1990). The campaigns I have chosen offer a reasonably succinct illustration of logics that were almost certainly important elsewhere too.

6. This is not to say that there were not other considerations that played a part too. It is usually agreed that general reform of the legal system was also important, as was the increased significance of movable property over land and the vagaries of nineteenth-century economic life (Holcombe, 1980; Shanley, 1989, pp. 15–17). Nevertheless, as Holcombe points out, reforms were bitterly resisted and took over 25 years to achieve and arguments based on liberal principles were extremely important in gaining legitimacy for the changes that were introduced.

7. Although there has been extensive research on suffragism there has been relatively little on the ideas of the movement in Britain (Holton, 1986, p. 9). Among those that do deal with ideas, which are drawn on in this section are: Garner (1984); Holton (1986); Maynard (1989); Rover (1967, chs 4 and 5); Bacchi (1990, pp. 19–28).

8. According to Sandra Holton, the analogy with economic class was significant; the suffrage movement managed to unite those for whom economic class was as important as sexual inequality, and who were therefore concerned with adult suffrage above all, with those for whom it was women's disenfranchisement that mattered most (Holton, 1986, pp. 7–8). Once the vote was won this unity was shattered and the movement split over the issue of which to give priority, sex or class (see also Phillips, 1987a, ch. 4).

9. Controversial as this reading of Mill's theory may be, I would refer the reader to the passages quoted in the previous section of this chapter. Also to an article by Susan Mendus, discovered after this was written, on how Mill's version of democracy allows for the inclusion of women as citizens without denying difference between the sexes in the name of equality (Mendus, 1993).

CHAPTER 5

1. This is not to say that there been no feminist treatment of twentieth-century liberal thinkers (see Okin, 1989; Frazer and Lacey, 1993). But those thinkers who had an important influence on political and social practices, the New Liberals on the welfare state and the neo-liberals on the New Right attempt to dismantle it, have generally not received feminist attention.

2. See also Clarke (1978); Collini (1979); Freeden (1978; 1986); Weiler (1982); Pugh (1993, ch. 6), Vincent and Plant (1984); Bentley (1987).

3. The theory of evolution led New Liberals to consider very seriously the eugenicist arguments current at the time they were writing. Although, as Hobson describes himself, biased towards environmental explanations of individual character traits, intelligence, etc. (Hobson, 1976, p. 151), such that most New Liberal arguments were designed to dampen the enthusiasm of more committed eugenicists, given also their interest in biological theories, New Liberals did suppose that the human 'stock' of a progressive society should be such that it would not impede that progress. To this end Hobhouse recommended that 'the feeble-minded' should not be permitted to reproduce, since to allow them to do so would clearly lead to deleterious effects and preventing them would not require measures incompatible with liberal freedoms (Hobhouse, 1968, p. 45). As far as I am aware, the New Liberals had no views specifically on the question of different peoples and nations as races; they were specifically interested in social evolution which they saw as distinct from biological evolution, involving the progress of rational self-determination, and they were not interested in the issue of racial development *per se*.

4. See also Fraser (1989); and Walby (1994).

There is also a sociological literature on the patriarchy of the welfare state which is specifically concerned with how private patriarchy – the appropriation of a woman's services by an individual man in the home – has given way to public patriarchy – women are now frequently likely to be economically dependent on, and controlled by, the state, rather than an individual man (either as clients or employees). There are various versions of this thesis, which I will not go into, but to summarise, the system is seen as patriarchal, first, because women are still disadvantaged in relation to men – they are more likely to be in poverty; second, because men benefit from their labour which serves to reproduce the workforce; and third, because they are not involved in making the major decisions that affect their lives as a result of their exclusion from the political process: Hernes (1984); Siim (1988); Walby (1990); Brown (1981). Since we are particularly concerned with the legitimating principles of gender inequalties in the welfare state, rather than the structure of its institutions *per se*, we shall not consider this literature here. Pateman's analysis is somewhat different from that of 'public patriarchy' theorists in so far as she is concerned with how the welfare state upholds traditional 'private' patriarchy as well as instituting a form of second-class citizenship for women. My analysis is not in disagreement with this literature except insofar as I do not see the state as monolithically patriarchal: although women's citizenship is inferior, the welfare state is nevertheless also emancipatory and has the potential to be more so.

5. According to Pateman men are 'independent' in three ways in which women are not: they have the capacity to use force, for self-protection and the protection of the state while women are 'protected' by men; they own property in their own persons while women continue to the property of men in some respects (for example, she says, rape in marriage is legally impossible in some states of the US and Australia and in Britain, but note that in Britain, at least, this is no longer the case); men are self-governing

as breadwinners while women are subordinate as dependants of men (pp. 185–7). This last type of independence is most important since, she argues, the main criteria of full citizenship is employment (p. 184).

6. The private sphere of 'personal liberties' is not exactly identical to the private domestic sphere even in terms of insurance provision. Beveridge was very keen to allow for the continuation of voluntary insurance, and especially of the already existing cooperative insurance schemes (Beveridge, 1966, pp. 143–5). And women cannot be seen as undecidable in relation to *this* opposition between public and private (which is anyway not rigorous since 'private' insurance schemes were to be closely regulated by the state and were not to be run as profitable enterprises). 'Women' as an undecidable is only constitutive of the opposition between the public sphere of state and civil society and the private domestic sphere insofar as the latter is equivalent to the private sphere of 'personal liberties', which it is only to a limited extent.

7. Beveridge specifically coins this term to replace the terminology of previous insurance schemes which described women as dependants. Women are not to be so described, he argues, because this detracts from the valuable work they do in their own right as wives and mothers (p. 49).

8. In fact, contrary to Beveridge's proposals, when the scheme was introduced married women seem to have paid either reduced contributions for reduced benefits, or full contributions for reduced benefits but pension rights as individuals (Atkins and Hoggett, 1984, pp. 165–6).

9. This point refers *only* to the private domestic sphere; as noted above, Beveridge was also anxious to make provision for private voluntary insurance schemes outside the national scheme. In practice, however, these had little success.

10. Among the exceptions are that women can claim for dependants only if their partner's income is below a certain level (Campbell and Coote, 1987, p. 91), differences in retirement ages remain unchanged (though they are now under review) and men are not eligible for a widower's pension (Johnson, 1990, pp. 55–6).

11. Interestingly, wages for women's work in the home to be paid by the state were one of the proposals of feminist critics of the Beveridge Report in the 1940s. Such payment, they argued, would be a real recognition of the value of women's contribution to the community (Clarke et al., 1987, pp. 103–4).

12. Permissive legislation involved the retreat of the law as a moral force in such activities as gambling, suicide, obscenity and censorship, abortion and divorce. Although the legislation was passed piecemeal by private members, and although each reform had a long history of campaigning behind it, it was unified insofar as it was encouraged by 'revisionists' in the Labour Party who were attempting to displace the old socialist image of the party with a new social vision of freedom designed to capture the votes of the growing ranks of young professionals, technocrats and 'embourgeoisified' workers. They failed to achieve hegemony in the party and parliamentary majorities were not guaranteed, but they did contribute to a relatively favourable climate for moral reform (Weeks, 1981, pp. 264–8).

According to Martin Durham, 'progressive Tories' were also favourable and sensitive to the electoral appeal of a 'modernising' liberal approach (Durham, 1991, pp. 6–7).

13. There have been changes in legislation concerning divorce since the 1960s notably the emphasis on 'clean break' divorce since 1984, where couples make a final settlement at the moment of divorce. But as long as there are children, courts still intervene to ensure arrangements for their welfare (Douglas, 1990, pp. 414–16). And it seems unlikely that the Children Act 1989 will reduce this. Although it provides for couples to make their own arrangements outside court for children's welfare so that courts are no longer required to pass judgements on these arrangements before granting the decree, they may intervene if the child him/herself is unhappy with these arrangements or if they are contested by any interested party, including relatives outside the nuclear family (Parton, 1991, pp. 153–4; Hoggett, 1993).

14. This should not be seen in reductionist terms as simply a matter of economics – the fact that the market needs low-paid, part-time workers and that women do these jobs (Barrett and McIntosh, 1991, p. 13; Lovenduski and Randall, 1993, pp. 43–4). By the mid-1980s the view that one way to solve unemployment would be to get women out of the labour force and back into the home was 'unsayable' in public (it *was* sayable in the Family Policy Group whose minutes were leaked in 1983) (Campbell, 1987, p. 175) and this must be understood as a construction of the limits within which the economic crisis could be addressed, rather than as a straightforward response to economic facts.

CONCLUSION

1. I am aware that this study has barely addressed the issue of differences between women. In the case of the differences between white and black women this is in part as a result of the taken-for-granted whiteness of the traditions with which it has been concerned. Liberalism, as we have seen, is concerned for the most part with disembodied individuals, and it is only where feminists have used the constitutive undecidability of its use of women that it has taken women's specificity into account. For most of its history, feminism has taken white women as the norm and has not considered the specificity of the position of black women and this is reflected in the analysis of feminist campaigns in previous chapters. It is only in recent years that the claims of black feminists have been taken up by white feminists and since the study is not intended to be a comprehensive history of feminism, they have not been considered here. It would perhaps be possible to analyse the relation of black women to the constitutive undecidability of women in liberalism but this would be another study.

References

Addison, P. (1994) *The Road to 1945: British Politics and the Second World War*, 2nd edn, London: Pimlico.

Alberti, J. (1996) *Eleanor Rathbone*, London: Sage.

Arblaster, A. (1984) *The Rise and Decline of Western Liberalism*, Oxford: Basil Blackwell.

Arblaster, A. (1987) *Democracy*, Milton Keynes: Open University Press.

Ashby, M. (1968) *The Glorious Revolution of 1688*, London: Panther.

Astell, M. (1986a) 'Reflections Upon Marriage', in B. Hill, *The First English Feminist: Reflections Upon Marriage and other Writings by Mary Astell*, Gower, Aldershot.

Astell, M. (1986b) 'A Serious Proposal', in B. Hill, *The First English Feminist: Reflections Upon Marriage and other Writings by Mary Astell*, Gower, Aldershot.

Atkins, S. and Hoggett, B. (1984) *Women and the Law*, Oxford: Basil Blackwell.

Bacchi, C. (1990) *Same Difference: Feminism and Sexual Difference*, London: Allen and Unwin.

Baier, A. (1987) 'The Need for More than Justice', in M. Hanen and K. Nielson, *Science, Morality and Feminist Theory*, University of Calgary Press, Calgary, Alberta.

Baldock, J. and Ungerson, C. (1991) 'What d'ya want if you don' want money? A Feminist Critique of "Paid Volunteering"', in M. Maclean and D. Groves, *Women's Issues in Social Policy*, Routledge, London.

Banks, O. (1981) *Faces of Feminism: A Study of Feminism as a Social Movement*, Oxford: Martin Robertson.

Barrett, M. and McIntosh, M. (1991) *The Anti-Social Family*, 2nd edn, London: Verso.

Barrett, M. and Phillips, A. (eds) (1992) *Destabilizing Theory: Contemporary Feminist Debates*, Cambridge: Polity.

Bellamy, R. (ed.) (1990) *Victorian Liberalism: Nineteenth Century Political Thought and Practice*, London: Routledge.

Bellamy, R. (1992) *Liberalism and Modern Society: An Historical Argument*, Cambridge: Polity.

Benhabib, S. (1987) 'The Generalised and the Concrete Other: the Kohlberg-Gilligan Controversy and Moral Theory', in E.F. Kittay and D.T. Meyers, *Women and Moral Theory*, Rowman and Littlefield, Totowa, New Jersey.

Bentley, M. (1987) *The Climax of Liberal Politics: British Liberalism in Theory and Practice 1868–1918*, London: Edward Arnold.

Beveridge, W. (1949) 'Epilogue' to E. Rathbone, *Family Allowances*, London: George Allen and Unwin.

Beveridge, W. (1966) *Social Insurance and Allied Services*, London: Her Majesty's Stationery Office.

Beveridge, W. (1986) 'Why am I a Liberal?', in R. Eccleshall, *British Liberalism: Liberal Thought from the 1640s to the 1980s*, Longman, London.

Bock, G. and James, S. (eds) (1992) *Beyond Equality and Difference: Citizenship, Feminist Politics and Female Subjectivity*, London: Routledge.

Bock, G. and Thane, P. (eds) (1991) *Maternity and Gender Policies: Women and the Rise of the European Welfare States, 1880s–1950s*, London: Routledge.

Bouchier, D. (1983) *The Feminist Challenge: The Movement for Women's Liberation in Britain and the USA*, London: Macmillan.

Brennan, T. and Pateman, C. (1979) 'Mere Auxiliaries to the Commonwealth: Women and the Origns of Liberalism', in *Political Studies*, 27/2.

Broughton, J. (1983) 'Women's Rationality and Men's Virtues', in *Social Research*, 50/3, Autumn.

Brown, C. (1981) 'Mothers, Fathers and Children: From Private to Public Patriarchy', in *Women and Revolution: A Discussion of the Unhappy Marriage of Marxism and Feminism*, South End Press, Boston, Mass.

Bryson, V. (1992) *Feminist Political Theory: An Introduction*, London: Macmillan.

Bulpitt, J. (1986) 'The Discipline of the New Democracy: Mrs Thatcher's Domestic Statecraft', *Political Studies*, vol. 34.

Burman, S. (ed.) (1979) *Fit Work for Women*, London: Croom Helm.

Butler, J. (1990) *Gender Trouble: Feminism and the Subversion of Identity*, London: Routledge.

Butler, J. (1994) 'Gender as Performance: An Interview with Judith Butler', in *Radical Philosophy*, no. 67, Summer.

Campbell, B. (1987) *Iron Ladies: Why do Women Vote Tory?*, London: Virago.

Carter, A. (1988) *The Politics of Women's Rights*, London: Longman.

Caverero, A. (1992) 'Equality and Sexual Difference: Amnesia in Political Thought', in G. Bock and S. James, *Beyond Equality and Difference: Citizenship, Feminist Politics and Female Subjectivity*, London: Routledge.

Charvet, J. (1982) *Feminism*, London: J.M. Dent.

Chodorow, N. (1978) *The Reproduction of Mothering: Psychoanalysis and the Sociology of Gender*, Berkley, California: University of California Press.

Clarke, J. Cochrane, A. and Smart, C. (eds) (1987) *Ideologies of Welfare: From Dreams to Disillusion*, London: Hutchinson.

Clarke, P. (1978) *Liberals and Social Democrats*, Cambridge: Cambridge University Press.

Collini, S. (1979) *Liberalism and Sociology: L.T. Hobhouse and Political Argument in England 1880–1914*, Cambridge: Cambridge University Press.

Connolly, W. (1992) *Identity/Difference: Democratic Negotiations of Political Paradox*, Ithaca, New York: Cornell University Press.

Coole, D. (1988) *Women in Political Theory: From Ancient Misogyny to Contemporary Feminism*, Hemel Hempstead, Herts: Harvester Wheatsheaf.

Coote, A. and Campbell, B. (1987) *Sweet Freedom: The Struggle for Women's Liberation*, 2nd edn, Oxford: Basil Blackwell.

Cornell, D. (1991) *Beyond Accommodation: Ethical Feminism, Deconstruction and the Law*, London: Routledge.

Corr, H. and Jamieson, L. (eds) (1990) *Politics of Everyday Life: Continuity and Change in Work and the Family*, London: Macmillan.

Corrigan, P. and Sayer, D. (1985) *The Great Arch: English State Formation as Cultural Revolution*, Oxford: Basil Blackwell.

Dale, J. and Foster, P. (1986) *Feminists and State Welfare*, London: Routledge and Kegan Paul.

Derrida, J. (1981a) 'The Double Session', in *Disseminations*, trans. B. Johnson, London: The Athlone Press.

Derrida, J. (1981b) *Positions*, trans. A. Bass, London: The Athlone Press.

Derrida, J. (1988) *Ltd Inc*, Evanston, Illinois: Northwestern University Press.

Derrida, J. (1991) 'Choreographies', in P. Kamuf, *A Derrida Reader: Between the Blinds*, Hemel Hampstead, Herts: Harvester Wheatsheaf.

Distefano, C. (1991) *Configurations of Masculinity: A Feminist Perspective on Modern Political Theory*, Ithaca, New York: Cornell University Press.

Donzelot, J. (1979) *The Policing of the Family: Welfare versus the State*, London: Hutchinson.

Douglas, G. (1990) 'Family Law under the Thatcher Government', *Journal of Law and Society*, 17/4, Winter.

Dunn, J. (ed.) (1993) *Democracy: the Unfinished Journey* Oxford: Oxford University Press.

Durham, M. (1991) *Sex and Politics: the Family and Morality in the Thatcher Years*, London: Macmillan.

Eccleshall, R. (ed.) (1986) *British Liberalism: Liberal Thought from the 1640s to the 1980s*, London: Longman.

Eisenstein, H. (1984) *Contemporary Feminist Thought*, London: Unwin Paperbacks.

Eisenstein, Z. (1981) *The Radical Future of Liberal Feminism*, New York: Longman.

Elshtain, J. (1981) *Public Man, Private Woman: Women in Social and Political Thought*, Oxford: Martin Robertson.

Elshtain, J. (ed.) (1982) *The Family in Political Thought*, Brighton: Harvester Press.

Evans, J., Hills, J., Hunt, K., Meehan, E., Ten Tusscher, T., Vogel, U. and Waylen, G. (1986) *Feminism and Political Theory*, London: Sage.

Ferguson, M. (1985) *First Feminists: British Women Writers 1578–1799*, Bloomington, Indiana: Indiana University Press.

Filmer, R. (1991) *Patriarcha and Other Writings*, ed. J.P. Sommerville, Cambridge: Cambridge University Press.

Foucault, M. (1972) *The Archaeology of Knowledge*, trans. A. Sheridan, London: Tavistock.

Fox-Genovese, E. (1991) *Feminism without Illusions: A Critique of Individualism*, London: University of Carolina Press.

Fraser, N. (1989) 'Women, Welfare and the Politics of Need Interpretation', in *Unruly Practices: Power, Discourse and Gender in Contemporary Social Theory*, Cambridge: Polity.

Fraser, N. and Nicholson, L. (1990) 'Social Criticism without Philosphy: An Encounter between Feminism and Postmodernism', in L. Nicholson, *Feminism/Postmodernism*, London: Routledge.

Frazer, E. and Lacey, N. (1993) *The Politics of Community: A Feminist Critique of the Liberal-Communitarian Debate*, Hemel Hampstead, Herts: Harvester Wheatsheaf.

Frazer, E., Hornsby, J. and Lovibond, S. (eds) (1992) *Ethics: A Feminist Reader*, Oxford: Basil Blackwell.

Freeden, M. (1978) *The New Liberalism: An Ideology of Social Reform*, Oxford: Clarendon Press.

Freeden, M. (1986) *Liberalism Divided: A Study in British Political Thought 1914–39*, Oxford: Clarendon Press.

Freeden, M. (1990) 'The New Liberalism and its Aftermath', in R. Bellamy, *Victorian Liberalism: Nineteenth Century Political Thought and Practice*, London: Routledge.

Friedman, M. (1987a) 'Beyond Caring: the De-moralization of Gender', in M. Hanen and K. Nielson, *Science, Morality and Feminist Theory*, Calgary, Alberta: University of Calgary Press.

Friedman, M. (1987b) 'Care and Context in Moral Reasoning', in E.F. Kittay and D.T. Meyers (eds), *Women and Moral Theory*, Tototwa, New Jersey: Rowman & Littlefield.

Gamble, A. (1986) 'The Political Economy of Freedom', in R. Levitas, *The Ideology of the New Right*, Cambridge: Polity.

Gardiner, J. (1983) 'Women, Recession and the Tories', in S. Hall and M. Jacques (eds), *The Politics of Thatcherism*, London: Lawrence & Wishart.

Garner, L. (1984) *Stepping Stones to Women's Liberty: Feminist Ideas in the Women's Suffrage Movement 1900–1918*, London: Heinemann.

Gasche, R. (1986) *The Tain of the Mirror: Derrida and the Philosophy of Reflection*, Cambridge, Mass: Harvard University Press.

Gatens, M. (1991a) 'A Critique of the Sex/Gender Distinction', in S. Gunew, *A Reader in Feminist Knowledge*, London: Routledge.

Gatens, M. (1991b) *Feminism and Philosophy: Perspectives on Difference and Equality*, Cambridge: Polity.

Gatens, M. (1992) 'Power, Bodies and Difference', in M. Barrett and A. Phillips, *Destabilizing Theory: Contemporary Feminist Debates*, Cambridge: Polity.

Gilligan, C. (1982) *In a Different Voice: Psychological Theory and Women's Development*, Cambridge, Mass: Harvard University Press.

Gilligan, C. (1986) 'Reply by Carol Gilligan', in *Signs* 11/2.

Goodin, R. and Pettit, P. (eds) (1993) *A Companion to Contemporary Political Philosophy*, Oxford: Basil Blackwell.

Goreau, A. (1985) *The Whole Duty of a Woman: Female Writers in Seventeenth Century England*, New York: The Dial Press.

Greeno, C. and Maccoby, E. (1986) 'How Different is the "Different Voice"?' in *Signs*, 11/2, Winter.

Gunew, S. (ed.) (1991) *A Reader in Feminist Knowledge*, London: Routledge.

Hall, S. (1983) 'The Great Moving Right Picture Show', in S. Hall and M. Jacques, *The Politics of Thatcherism*, London: Lawrence and Wishart.

Hall, S. and Jacques, M. (eds) (1983) *The Politics of Thatcherism*, London: Lawrence and Wishart.

Hall, S., Critcher, C., Jefferson, T., Clarke, J. and Roberts, B. (1978) *Policing the Crisis: Mugging, the State and Law and Order*, London: Macmillan.

Hanen, M. and Nielson, K. (eds) (1987) *Science, Morality and Feminist Theory*, Calgary, Alberta: University of Calgary Press.

Harris, J. (1977) *William Beveridge: A Biography*, Oxford: Clarendon Press.

Harrison, B. (1978) *Separate Spheres: The Opposition to Women's Suffrage in Britain*, London: Croom Helm.

Held, D. (1987) *Models of Democracy*, Cambridge: Polity.

Held, D. (1991) *Political Theory Today*, Cambridge: Polity.

Held, D. (1993) (ed) *Prospects for Democracy: North, South, East, West*, Cambridge: Polity.

Held, D. and Pollitt, C. (eds) (1986) *New Forms of Democracy*, London: Sage.

Hernes, H. (1984) 'Women and the Welfare State: The Transition from Private to Public Dependence', in H. Holter, *Patriarchy in a Welfare Society*, Oslo: Universitetsforlaget.

Hill, B. (1986) *The First English Feminist: Reflections Upon Marriage and other writings by Mary Astell*, Aldershot: Gower.

Hirst, P. (1994) *Associative Democracy: New Forms of Economic and Social Governance*, Cambridge: Polity.

Hobhouse, L.T. (1904) *Democracy and Reaction*, London: T. Fisher Unwin.

Hobhouse, L.T. (1968) *Social Evolution and Political Theory*, Port Washington, New York: Kennicat Press.

Hobhouse, L.T. (1994) *Liberalism and Other Writings*, ed. J. Meadowcraft, Cambridge: Cambridge University Press.

Hobson, J.A. (1909) *The Crisis of Liberalism: New Issues of Democracy*, London: P.S. King and Co.

Hobson, J.A. (1976) *Confessions of an Economic Heretic*, ed. M. Freeden, Brighton: Harvester Press.

Hoggett, B. (1993) *Parents and Children*, 4th edition, London: Sweet & Maxwell.

Holcombe, L. (1980) 'Victorian Wives and Property: Reform of the Married Woman's Property Law 1857–1882', in M. Vicinus, *Suffer and Be Still: Women in the Victorian Age*, Bloomington, Indiana: Indiana University Press.

Hollis, P. (ed.) (1979) *Women in Public 1850–1900: Documents of the Victorian Women's Movement*, London: George Allen and Unwin.

Holter, H. (ed.) (1984) *Patriarchy in a Welfare Society*, Oslo: Universitetsforlaget.

Holton, S. (1986) *Feminism and Democracy: Women's Suffrage and Reform Politics in Britain 1900–1918*, Cambridge: Cambridge University Press.

Jessop, B., Ling, S., Bonnet, K. and Bromley, K. (1988) 'Authoritarian Populism, Two Nations and Thatcherism', in B. Jessop, S. Ling, K. Bonnet and K. Bromley, *Thatcherism: A Tale of Two Nations*, Cambridge: Polity.

Johnson, N. (1990) *Reconstructing the Welfare State: A Decade of Change 1980–90*, Hemel Hampstead, Herts: Harvester and Wheasheaf.

Jones, K. and Jonasdottir, A. (eds) (1988) *The Political Interests of Gender: Developing Theory and Research with a Feminist Face*, London: Sage.

Jones, B., Gray A., Kavanagh, D., Moran M., Norton, P. and Seldon, A. (1991) *Politics UK*, Hemel Hampstead, Herts: Phillip Allan.

Kamuf, P. (1991) *A Derrida Reader: Between the Blinds*, Hemel Hempstead, Herts: Harvester Wheatsheaf.

Keane, J. (1988) *Democracy and Civil Society: On the Predicaments of European Socialism, the Prospects for Democracy, and the Problem of Controlling Social and Political Power*, London: Verso.

Kent, S. (1990) *Sex and Suffrage in Britain 1850–1914*, London: Routledge.

Keown, J. (1988) *Abortion, Doctors and the Law: Some Aspects of the Legal Regulation of Abortion in England from 1803 to 1982*, Cambridge: Cambridge University Press.

Kittay, E.F. and Meyers, D.T. (eds) (1987) *Women and Moral Theory*, Totowa, New Jersey: Rowman and Littlefield.

Kohlberg, L., with Levine, C. and Hewer, A. (1984) 'Moral Stages: A Current Statement and Response to Critics', in L. Kohlberg, *Essays on Moral Development*, vol. 2: *The Psychology of Moral Development*, New York: Harper and Row.

Koven, S. (1993) 'Borderlands: Women, Voluntary Action, and Child Welfare in Britain 1840 to 1914', in S. Koven and S. Michel, *Mothers of a New World: Maternalist Politics and the Origins of Welfare States*, New York: Routledge.

Koven, S. and Michel, S. (eds) (1993) *Mothers of a New World: Maternalist Politics and the Origins of Welfare States*, New York: Routledge.

Kraditor, A. (1981) *The Ideas of the Woman Suffrage Movement 1890–1920*, New York: W.W. Norton and Co.

Krouse, R. (1982) 'Patriarchal Liberalism and Beyond: From John Stuart Mill to Harriet Taylor', in J. Elshtain, *The Family in Political Thought*, Brighton: Harvester Press.

Kymlicka, W. (1989) *Liberalism, Community, and Culture*, Oxford: Oxford University Press.

Kymlicka, W. (1990) *Contemporary Political Philosophy: An Introduction*, Oxford: Oxford University Press.

Laclau, E. (1990) *New Reflections on the Revolution of Our Time*, London: Verso.

Laclau, E. (1993a) 'Discourse', in R. Goodin and P. Pettit, *A Companion to Contemporary Political Philosophy*, Oxford: Basil Blackwell.

Laclau, E. (1993b) 'Power and Representation', in M. Poster, *Politics, Theory and Contemporary Culture*, New York: Columbia University Press.

Laclau, E. and Mouffe, C. (1985) *Hegemony and Socialist Strategy: Toward a Radical Democratic Politics*, London: Verso.

Land, H. (1991) 'Time to Care', in M. Maclean and D. Groves, *Women's Issues in Social Policy*, London: Routledge.

Laslett, P. (1971) *The World We Have Lost*, 2nd edition, London: Methuen.

Lefort, C. (1986) *The Political Forms of Modern Society: Bureaucracy, Democracy, Totalitarianism*, ed. J. Thompson, Cambridge: Polity.

Lefort, C. (1988) *Democracy and Political Theory*, trans. D. Macey, Cambridge: Polity.

Levine, P. (1990) *Feminist Lives in Victorian England: Private Roles and Public Commitment*, Oxford: Basil Blackwell.

Levitas, R. (ed.) (1986) *The Ideology of the New Right*, Cambridge: Polity.

Lewis, J. (ed.) (1979) *Before the Vote was Won: Arguments for and against Women's Suffrage*, London: Routledge and Kegan Paul.

Lewis, J. (1987) 'Feminism and Welfare', in J. Mitchell and A. Oakley, *What is Feminism?*, Oxford: Basil Blackwell.

Lewis, J. (1991) 'Models of Equality for Women: The Case of State Support for Children in Twentieth Century Britain', in G. Bock and P. Thane, *Maternity and Gender Policies: Women and the Rise of the European Welfare States, 1880s–1950s*, London: Routledge.

Lewis, J. (1992) *Women in Britain since 1945*, Oxford: Basil Blackwell.

Lewis, J. (1994) 'Gender, the Family and Women's Agency in the Building of "Welfare States": The British Case', in *Social History* 19/1.

Locke, J. (1960) *Two Treatises of Government*, ed. P. Laslett, Cambridge: Cambridge University Press.

Loney, R., Bocock, R., Clarke, J., Cochrane, A., Graham, P. and Wilson, M. (eds) (1991) *The State or the Market: Politics and Welfare in Contemporary Britain*, London: Sage.

Lovenduski, J. and Randall, V. (1993) *Contemporary Feminist Politics*, Oxford: Oxford University Press.

Luria, Z. (1986) 'A Methodological Critique', in *Signs* 11/2.

Poster, M. (ed.) (1993) *Politics, Theory and Contemporary Culture*, New York: Columbia University Press.

Maclean, M. and Groves, D. (eds) (1991) *Women's Issues in Social Policy*, London: Routledge.

Macpherson, C.B. (1977) *The Life and Times of Liberal Democracy*, Oxford: Oxford University Press.

Maynard, M. (1989) 'Privilege and Patriarchy in Feminist Thought in the Nineteenth Century', in S. Mendus and J. Rendell, *Sexuality and Subordination: Interdisciplinary Studies of Gender in the Nineteenth Century*, London: Routledge.

Mendus, S. (1993) 'Losing the Faith: Feminism and Democracy', in J. Dunn, *Democracy: the Unfinished Journey*, Oxford: Oxford University Press.

Mendus, S. and Rendell, J. (eds) (1989) *Sexuality and Subordination: Interdisciplinary Studies of Gender in the Nineteenth Century*, London: Routledge.

Mill, J.S. (1946) 'Considerations on Representative Government', in *On Liberty and Considerations on Representative Government*, ed. R.B. McCallum, Oxford: Basil Blackwell.

Mill, J.S. (1973) *J.S. Mill: Essays on Politics and Culture*, ed. G. Himmelfarb, Gloucester, Mass: Peter Smith.

Mill, J.S. (1973a) 'Tocqueville on Democracy in America', in *J.S. Mill: Essays on Politics and Culture*, ed. G. Himmelfarb, Gloucester, Mass: Peter Smith.

Mill, J.S. (1973b) 'Thoughts on Parliamentary Reform', in *J.S. Mill: Essays on Politics and Culture*, ed. G. Himmelfarb, Gloucester, Mass: Peter Smith.

Mill, J.S. (1989) *On Liberty with The Subjection of Women and Chapters on Socialism*, ed. S. Collini, Cambridge: Cambridge University Press.

Mill, J.S. (1989a) *On Liberty in On Liberty with The Subjection of Women and Chapters on Socialism* ed. S. Collini, Cambridge: Cambridge University Press.

Mill, J.S. (1989b) *The Subjection of Women in On Liberty with The Subjection of Women and Chapters on Socialism* ed. S. Collini, Cambridge: Cambridge University Press.

Mitchell, J. (1987) 'Women and Equality', in A. Phillips, *Feminism and Equality* Oxford: Basil Blackwell.

Mitchell, J. and Oakley, A. (eds) (1987) *What is Feminism?*, Oxford: Basil Blackwell.

Mouffe, C. (1993) *Return of the Political*, London: Verso.

Mouffe, C. (1993a) 'Radical Democracy: Modern or Postmodern?' in C. Mouffe, *Return of the Political*, London: Verso.

Mouffe, C. (1993b) 'Pluralism and Modern Democracy: Around Schmidt', in C. Mouffe, *Return of the Political*, London: Verso.

Nash, K. (forthcoming) 'Beyond Liberalism? Feminist Theories of Democracy', in V. Randall and G. Waylen, *Gender, Politics and the State*, London: Routledge.

Nicholson, L. (1986) *Gender and History: the Limits of Social Theory in the Age of the Family*, New York: Columbia University Press.

Nicholson, L. (ed.) (1990) *Feminism/Postmodernism*, London: Routledge.

Nicholson, L. (1983) 'Women, Morality and History', in *Social Research*, 50/3, Autumn.

Noddings, N. (1984) *Caring: A Feminine Approach to Ethics and Moral Education*, Berkeley, Calif.: University of California Press.

Oakley, A. (1985) *Sex, Gender and Society*, 2nd edn, Aldershot, Hants: Gower.

O'Donovan, K. (1985) *Sexual Divisions in Law*, London: Weidenfeld and Nicolson.

Okin, S. (1980) *Women in Western Political Thought*, London: Virago.

Okin, S. (1989) *Justice, Gender and the Family*, New York: Basic Books.

Okin, S. (1991) 'Gender, the Public and the Private', in D. Held, *Political Theory Today*, Cambridge: Polity.

Parton, N. (1991) *Governing the Family*, London: Macmillan.

Pateman, C. (1986) Introduction to Pateman and Gross (1986).

Pateman, C. and Gross, E. (1986) *Feminist Challenges: Social and Political Theory*, London: Allen and Unwin.

Pateman, C. (1988) *The Sexual Contract*, Cambridge: Polity.

Pateman, C. (1989) *The Disorder of Women: Democracy, Feminism and Political Theory*, Cambridge: Polity.

Pateman, C. (1989a) 'The Patriarchal Welfare State', in *The Disorder of Women: Democracy, Feminism and Political Theory*, Cambridge: Polity.

Pateman, C. (1989b) 'Feminist Critiques of the Public/Private Dichotomy' in *The Disorder of Women: Democracy, Feminism and Political Theory*, Cambridge: Polity.

Perry, R. (1986) *The Celebrated Mary Astell: An Early English Feminist*, Chicago, Illinois: The University of Chicago Press.

Phillips, A. (ed.) (1987a) *Feminism and Equality*, Oxford: Basil Blackwell.

Phillips, A. (1987b) *Divided Loyalties: Dilemmas of Sex and Class*, London: Virago.

Phillips, A. (1991) *Engendering Democracy*, Cambridge: Polity.

Phillips, A. (1992) 'Universal Pretensions in Political Thought', in M. Barrett and A. Phillips, *Destabilizing Theory: Contemporary Feminist Debates*, Cambridge: Polity.

Phillips, A. (1993a) 'Must Feminists Give Up on Liberal Democracy?' in D. Held, *Prospects for Democracy: North, South, East, West*, Cambridge: Polity.

Phillips, A. (1993b) *Democracy and Difference*, Cambridge: Polity.

Poster, M. (ed.) (1993) *Politics, Theory and Contemporary Culture*, New York: Columbia University Press.

Prochaska, F. (1980) *Women and Philanthropy in Nineteenth Century England*, Oxford: Clarendon Press.

Pugh, M. (1992) *Women and the Women's Movement in Britain 1914–59*, London: Macmillan.

Pugh, M. (1993) *The Making of Modern British Politics 1837–1939*, Oxford: Basil Blackwell.

Rathbone, E. (1949) *Family Allowances*, London: George Allen and Unwin.

Randall, V. and Waylen, G. (eds) (forthcoming) *Gender, Politics and the State*, London: Routledge.

Rendall, J. (1987) '"A Moral Engine"? Feminism, Liberalism and the *English Woman's Journal*', in *Women's Politics 1800–1914*, ed. J. Rendell, Oxford: Basil Blackwell.

Richards, J. (1982) *The Sceptical Feminist: A Philosophical Inquiry*, Harmondsworth: Penguin Books.

Riley, D. (1988) *Am I That Name?: Feminism and the Category of 'Women' in History*, London: Macmillan.

Ritchie, D.G. (1891) *Principles of State Interference*, London: Swann Sonnenschein and Co.

Rose, J. (1983) 'Femininity and its Discontents', in *Feminist Review*, 14, June.

Rover, C. (1967) *Women's Suffrage and Party Politics in Britain 1866–1914*, London: Routledge and Kegan Paul.

Rowbotham, S. (1986) 'Feminism and Democracy', in D. Held and C. Pollitt, *New Forms of Democracy*, London: Sage.

Rowbotham, S. (1989) *The Past is Before Us: Feminism in Action since the 1960s*, London: Penguin Books.

Ruggiero, G. (1959) *The History of European Liberalism*, trans. R. Collingwood, Boston, Mass: Beacon Press.

Sargent, L. (1981) *Women and Revolution: A Discussion of the Unhappy Marriage of Marxism and Feminism*, Boston, Mass: South End Press.

Schochet, G. (1975) *Patriarchalism in Political Thought: The Authoritarian Family and Political Speculation and Attitudes, Especially in Seventeenth Century England*, Oxford: Basil Blackwell.

Segal, L. (1983) 'The Heat in the Kitchen', in S. Hall and M. Jacques, *The Politics of Thatcherism*, London: Lawrence and Wishart.

Segal, L. (1987) *Is the Future Female? Troubled Thoughts on Contemporary Feminism*, London: Virago.

Shanley, M. (1982) 'Marriage Contract and Socal Contract in Seventeenth-Century English Political Thought' in J. Elshtain, *The Family in Political Thought*, Brighton: Harvester Press.

Shanley, M. (1989) *Feminism, Marriage and the Law in Victorian England 1850–95*, London: I.B. Taurus.

Siim, B. (1988) 'Towards a Feminist Rethinking of the Welfare State', in K. Jones and A. Jonasdottir, *The Political Interests of Gender: Developing Theory and Research with a Feminist Face*, London: Sage.

Skinner, Q. (1988a) 'Some Problems in the Analysis of Political Thought and Action', in J. Tully, *Meaning and Context: Quentin Skinner and his Critics*, Cambridge: Polity.

Skinner, Q. (1988b) 'Meaning and Understanding in the History of Ideas', in J. Tully, *Meaning and Context: Quentin Skinner and his Critics*, Cambridge: Polity.

Smart, C. (1984) *The Ties That Bind: Law, Marriage and the Reproduction of Patriarchal Relations*, London: Routledge and Kegan Paul.

Smart, C. (1991) 'Securing the Family? Rhetoric and Policy in the Field of Social Security', in R. Loney et al., *The State or the Market: Politics and Welfare in Contemporary Britain*, London: Sage.

Smith, H. (1982) *Reason's Disciples: Seventeenth Century English Feminists*, Urbana, Illinois: University of Illinois Press.

Stocks, M. (1949) *Eleanor Rathbone: A Biography*, London: Victor Gollancz.

Summers, A. (1979) 'A Home from Home: Women's Philanthropic Work in the Nineteenth Century', in S. Burman, *Fit Work for Women*, London: Croom Helm.

Taylor, B. (1983) *Eve and the New Jerusalem: Socialism and Feminism in the C19th*, London: Virago.

Thane, P. (1993) 'Women in the British Labour Party and the Construction of State Welfare 1906–1939', in S. Koven and S. Michel, *Mothers of a New World: Maternalist Politics and the Origins of Welfare States*, New York: Routledge.

Tully, J. (1988) *Meaning and Context: Quentin Skinner and his Critics*, Cambridge: Polity.

Young, I. (1990) 'Impartiality and the Civic Public', in *Throwing Like a Girl and Other Essays in Philosophy and Social Theory*, Bloomington, Indiana: Indiana University Press.

Vicinus, M. (ed.) (1974) *Suffer and Be Still: Women in the Victorian Age*, Bloomington, Indiana: Indiana University Press.

Vincent, A. and Plant, R. (1984) *Philosophy, Politics and Citizenship: The Life and Thought of the British Idealists*, Oxford: Basil Blackwell.

Walby, S. (1990) 'Women's Employment and the Historical Periodization of Patriarchy', in H. Corr and L. Jamieson, *Politics of Everyday Life: Continuity and Change in Work and the Family*, London: Macmillan.

Walby, S. (1994) 'Is Citizenship Gendered?' in *Sociology*, 28/2, May.

Waylen, G. (1986) 'Women and Neo-liberalism', in J. Evans et al., *Feminism and Political Theory*, London: Sage.

Weber, M. (1982) 'The Social Psychology of the World Religions', *For Weber: Essays in Sociology*, ed. H. Gerth and C. Mills, London: Routledge.

Weeks, J. (1981) *Sex, Politics and Society: The Regulation of Sexuality since 1800*, London: Longman.

Weiler, P. (1982) *The New Liberalism: Liberal Social Theory in Great Britain 1889–1914*, London: Garland Publishing.

Wiesner, M. (1993) *Women and Gender in Early Modern Europe*, Cambridge: Cambridge University Press.

Williams, F. (1991) 'The Welfare State as Part of a Racially Structured and Patriarchal Capitalism', in R. Loney et al., *The State or the Market: Politics and Welfare in Contemporary Britain*, London: Sage.

Wollstonecraft, M. (1992) *Vindication of the Rights of Woman*, ed. M. Brody, London: Penguin Books.

Index